A Father's Son

by

Robert B. Marchand

Argus Enterprises International, Inc.
North Carolina***New Jersey

A Father's Son © 2011 All rights reserved by Robert B. Marchand

No part of this book may be reproduced or transmitted in any form or by any means, graphic, electronic, or mechanical, including photocopying, recording, taping, or by any informational storage retrieval system without prior permission in writing from the publisher.

A-Argus Better Book Publishers, LLC

For information:
A-Argus Better Book Publishers, LLC
9001 Ridge Hill Street
Kernersville, North Carolina 27285
www.a-argusbooks.com

ISBN: 978-0-6155076-8-2
ISBN: 0-6155076-8-9

Book Cover designed by Dubya

Printed in the United States of America

Dedication

A Father's Son is dedicated to two persons who haveseriously affected my life in a positive way. One of these persons was my Mother, who after many years of both physical and mental abuse, was finally able to stand her ground and declare her independence.

The other person is my wife Sharon, who tries so hard each and every day to show and teach me what love really is all about.

Author's Note

A Father's Son is a collection of true stories. The author, raised on a remotely located subsistence farm in Northern Ontario by a abusive father, relates in *A Fathers Son* many tales of the adventures that he experienced during his abused early formative years. While not dwelling extensively on the abuse he was subjected to during those long ago years, he does occasionally reveal some of these mental and physical abuses to the reader.Names, characters and places in A Fathers Son are either the product of the Authors imagination or used fictitiously. Any resemblance to actual locales, organizations or persons, living or dead, is entirely coincidental.

Introduction

Spring - 1945:

The father, Bazil Marlowe has just returned home to his wife Ruby, six-year-old daughter Doreen and his four-year-old son Bob after spending nearly five years inEngland, Sicily and Italy where he served as a medic in the Royal Canadian Medical Corps. During the early years of the war, he, along with thousands of other Canadian Military personnel, languished in England for two years while waiting for the Allies to begin the invasion of continental Europe. During this long wait he apparently, (according to relatives and the mother of young Bob) met, and co-habilitated with, a English girl with whom he stayed, until he was finally deployed to Sicily during the invasion. As related to his son, and through overheard conversations by relatives and from his mother much later in his life, he thought this arrangement was only fair as his Canadian wife (Bobs mother) had given birth to Bob approximately eleven months after he had joined the Canadian Military and shipped out for England, causing him to reason, rightly or wrongly, that the boy was not his real son. He thought this even though he had gone AWOL, as his Military records confirmed, and had visited his wife during the period immediately prior to his departure for England. He seemed to have conveniently forgotten that particular visit to his wife.

Marlowe served without distinction until the war ended in nineteen-forty-five, attaining the rank of Corporal. For some forgotten reason, he decided, after the war ended, to rejoin his wife and children who were, at that time, living in a little gold mining town in Northern Ontario. He then took his wife's four hundred dollars of savings that she had accumulated from her Government-issued children's allowance checks, and purchased a one-hundred and sixty acre dilapidated old farm in a area called "South Mindoka" that lay about sixteen miles south of town. He also took out homestead rights on an adjoining eighty acre parcel of forested land. The first property contained an old, run-down wood-frame, three-room, single story house that he then occupied with his wife, daughter and son whom he assumed, (and made quite clear to the boy and his mother over the next ten or so years) was his "bastard" son.

The following stories are, the true accountings of the upbringing of young Bob, Doreen and his other, yet-to-be-born, children on that old farm. The story does not attempt to justify, rationalize or explain the many physical and mental abuses that the Father bestowed upon his son Bob over the next twelve years. Sufficient to say that he was probably attempting, in some strange way, to punish his wife and his son for what he presumed were his wife's indiscretions during his long absence performing his Military Service in England and Europe.

Chapter 1

The Beginning

This true story begins in about nineteen forty-three in a small suburb of a Northern Ontario Town. My earliest recollections of these times are of living quite happily in a small house in the outskirts of this community with my mother and my older sister Doreen. My father was at this time in England, Spitzbergen or Italy with the Royal Canadian Army Medical Corps, tending the wounded and injured Canadian men wgi were fighting the German invaders.

This period of my young live is remembered by myself as the "good years." My Great-uncle Peter, brother of my mother's father, lived nearby and had assumed the father role to myself and my sister Doreen. He took us for many walks, let us ride on his dogsled during the long winter months, showed us the area's wildlife and generally acted out the father role to us kids during our real father's five year wartime absence in the far away war. My detailed memories of this time period are, for the most part, quite vague but I do recall moving to another nearby house where our family made friends with the next door neighbors. This family, the Lotts, was to eventually become lifelong friends of our family.

Uncle Peter, our Great-uncle, was a retired, unsuccessful prospector/trapper who finally gave up trying to find his own personal gold mine in the northern wilderness. He was now working in one of the towns many hard-rock underground gold mines. He owned at that time, two large dogs of some unknown breed that he had used as pack animals and for company when he was off in the northern wilderness searching for his ever elusive fortune. Great-uncle Peter was, as I was to find out much later in my life, also quite busy high-grading rich gold bearing ore from whichever mine he was working in at that time. He would take this rich ore with its readily visible gold into a hideout room in the basement of the house where he would place the rich pebbles of ore on a large metal anvil. He would then hammer away on them until all he had left was the soft malleable gold that he would quickly sell to a local buyer. Many, many years later, I still have, in a small glass vial, a few ounces of that high-graded, hammered yellow flattened gold that my Great-uncle Peter presented to my mother in those long ago days. Our family then moved once more to a more central location in our northern community where our Great-uncle Peter boarded with us prior to our father's return from war.

  I could later in my life barely recall any other event of that particular day, but I will always be able to readily recall the excitement of the day as the three of us anxiously awaited the steam train's arrival in the station. My first ever sight of my long gone father took place on a wooden railway platform in a small northern village called Swastika. Swastika was located about five miles west of the much larger gold mining town of Kirkland Lake in North-eastern Ontario. It was early spring of nineteen forty-five and the Second World War with the Germans had now finally concluded. Basil Marlowe, the soldier and the father whom I had never seen, and who, at the time, was my biggest hero, was finally returning home from the war that had occurred so far away. My mother, my six-year-old sister Doreen, (who I had, early in my life and much to her disgust, nicknamed "Diddy") and myself, at four years of age, were standing on that scarred old wooden platform waiting for the train and father's expected arrival home. I could, later in his life, barely recall any other events of that particular day but

A Father's Son

I will always be able to readily recall the excitement of the day as the three of us anxiously awaited the steam train's arrival in the station. My dad, my hero, the soldier who I had heard so much about during all of my young life, was finally coming home to us after over four long years of absence in the European war where he fought the evil Germans.

Up to that point in my young life I had never ever seen my soldier father. I had only seen pictures of a tall good looking, slim man dressed in a khaki Canadian Army uniform whom I was told was my father and who was in a different country far away and across the ocean, fighting the evil Germans. I had no idea at that time that my father did not believe that I was his legitimate birth son. Had I known, I probably would not, at my young age, have even understood just what that even meant. I did learn however, over the next five to eight years, through overheard conversations, and through my father's terrible treatment of me, that my father believed me to have been fathered by one of his younger brothers who had entered the war at a later date than he had.

When the puffing and belching steam train finally puffed into the little train station, my excitement reached new heights. My mother, my sister and I waited in eager anticipation as first; the conductor stepped off the train onto the platform and smiled down at us. After a few more seconds we saw a tall slim, uniformed man step down from the train a few cars away from where we stood waiting. We continued to wait as he walked towards us carrying a large khaki duffle bag. He was a good-looking, well-built soldier who I immediately knew was my daddy and my long gone war hero, home at last. As he neared us, my sister Doreen went forward to greet her father while I stood, waiting fearfully apprehensive, holding tightly onto my mother's hand as this tall stranger approached.. The tall soldier quickly scooped Doreen, my sister, up into his arms and hugging her tightly, smiled broadly and kissed her on her cheeks. As I anxiously awaited my turn for a similar such greeting from my father, he turned, gave our mother a quick peck on the cheek and then, carrying Doreen in his arms, strode away down the platform completely ignoring my presence. At that moment, just happy to finally see my father, I totally failed to grasp any real significance of what had just occurred. All I could recall later was thinking that this tall soldier was my father, my hero, and he was finally, at long last, home with us.

Shortly after our father's return from the war, our parents purchased an old, previously abandoned farm of one-hundred and sixty acres and took out homestead rights on adjoining eighty acres. The old farm had a ramshackle, dilapidated, three-room, un-insulated wood-frame house with weather-blackened wood siding, a weathered old log barn with a large hay loft, a small wooden shed and a old one-hole outhouse. This old farm and its structures were located on a dirt road about five-eighths of a mile from the nearest paved road, about five miles from the nearest food store and about sixteen miles from the nearest town. The house had no electric power, no plumbing whatsoever, no telephone, no heat, no insulation, single-pane windows, a leaky roof and was located, along with its one-hole outhouse and small shed, across a large ravine from the log barn and about twenty acres of partly cleared fields that had not seen a plow or any kind of cultivation for years. The houses only source of potable water was a shallow wood-encased well located about fifty yards from the house, across a deep ravine and part way up the other side of the far bank towards and just below the barn. It was equipped with a ancient hand-operated pump that required priming each time it was used. This was done with the water that was always kept in a pail at the well site for just that purpose. This was to be my home for the next fifteen or so years.

Over the next two or three years, the farm grew with the addition of three milk cows, a bull, two or three pigs, two horses, about one hundred chickens, a number of geese and ducks, and a beautiful collie dog that Doreen and I named Lassie, a house-cat and another young sister named Lynne. The old farmhouse also grew substantially in size over these next few years. Our mother's half-brother Larry and a local Finnish man called Mathew came to our parents' assistance and helped the couple add a second storey, a concrete chimney, a small ground level addition and a root cellar for the cool storage of our home-grown vegetables.

Our family could now boast of having a four-bedroom, two-story wood-frame, sawdust-insulated house with newly nailed on asphalt "brick-textured" siding. The house also now had a huge country kitchen with a large wood fired cook-stove that also served as the family's only water heater and a steel forty-five gallon barrel that had been converted into a wood heater in the family room. The concrete chimney straddled the upstairs bedrooms dividing wall and served as those two bedrooms' only source of heat. Besides the two upstairs bedrooms, the kitchen contained newly homemade, plywood kitchen cupboards, a porch and a large nearby woodshed. The family also had a brand new two-hole, much needed, and much closer, outhouse to serve the growing families toiletry needs. We were also, on a quite regular basis, to have the addition of three brothers, Don, Darren and Gil, all born in that old farmhouse in South Mindoka Township.

We were, in about nineteen fifty, to finally get electricity to our home, but never did have the money to bring in telephone lines or to get central heating. Our family's cooking and heating was always to be done with wood heaters and a wood cook-stove. It was not until the late fifties that we finally graduated from a large steel, "barrel-type" wood heater to a slightly smaller, but more efficient oil-fired space heater that was located, centrally, in our living room. More than sixty years later, I can still remember wakening in my cot on the many terribly cold winter mornings and seeing the thick layer of hoar frost adhering to and hanging in miniature icicles from the sloped, "ten-test" unpainted paneling of the ceiling that was directly over my head. This frost and little icicles had been caused by the frozen moisture of my breath, as I slept on my narrow little cot under a very thin threadbare blanket.

My father, in those early years following the Second World War, seemed to enjoy the self-sufficient wilderness farm life in rural Northern Ontario. The old farm, with much hard work, soon began to, relatively speaking, prosper. The family was growing, we were all reasonably healthy, we were never hungry, our huge garden seemed to grow everything that we planted, the farm animals and birds all reproduced regularly to provide all of our needed meats, eggs, pork and poultry. As everything appeared to be going well with the farm, our father decided that it was now time to diversify and that it was time to make some badly needed cash so our family could clear more land, purchase a car, a tractor, farm implements, more stock and other such items of luxury.

Our father soon purchased a small sawmill, a logging truck and a Massey-Harris tractor to power the sawmill and use for other farm chores. He also hired a local middle aged man of Finnish background, Mathew Dawson, to help in the logging of his heavily-timbered forest lands and to assist in the mill operations as well as other farm tasks. He also did custom lumber sawing for a local logging contractor who trucked in many loads of raw logs for him to saw into useable dimension lumber. He did quite well for himself and his growing family for a few years until he was suddenly stricken down by a severe case of rheumatoid arthritis that gradually affected his entire body. This terrible disease was to be the end of our father's dreams and the beginning of the end for the limited prosperity our family had enjoyed up to then. It was also the beginning of terrible times for our family as our father, with nothing constructive to do, and in constant pain, began to really vent his frustrations and his pent up anger on our mother and especially on me, his purported bastard son. The only fortunate thing to come out of his illness was that its cause was eventually attributed to an injury he had suffered during his wartime service. As a result, he was able to receive, for the remainder of his life, a small military disability pension. This pension, along with the government-issued small children's monthly family allowance checks were to be the only money that our family was to have for food, clothing and the other necessities of life.

The following stories are the true stories of an unhappy yet adventuresome young life and my ongoing struggles to live and to survive on a remote old Mindoka subsistence farm while striving to escape a terrible family life where the word love had no meaning whatsoever and as such was a word never heard or uttered in this dysfunctional family. It is the story of my pain, frustrations and suffering through years of physical and mental abuses as I grew to manhood, never truly understanding why my father seemed to hate and detest my very existence. I could never understand why my father used every possible means and opportunity to torment and to punish me both mentally and physically. I could never understand why my father found fault with everything I did or attempted to do. The story is however, not just a story of my pain and suffering. It is also the story of a young boy's wonderful adventures as I looked for and discovered myself, my personal aptitudes, developed my skills, formed my future and finally how I managed to escape from my father's abuses as I was forced to grow into manhood much sooner than was normal for any young boy in this rural Mindoka wilderness.

Chapter 2

The Early Years

The closest neighbors and good friends of my family when we lived in town were a family named Lott who lived, for a time, right next door to us. Ian and Barbara and their children, Patrick, Mary, Jon and Cheryl were to remain our good friends and our frequent visitors on the farm for many, many years. When the Lotts eventually moved further south to a town called North Bay, about one-hundred and forty miles south of New Liskeard they were seen much less frequently by us but they still remained good family friends. They did stay in touch with our family until Ian and Barbara finally passed away. They were very good friends and close neighbors of ours and were sorely missed on their passing. Many years later my younger sister Lynne, was to marry Jon Lott, the youngest son of Ian and Barbara. Jon was to become a hockey player and goalie that played professionally in the USA for a few years before marrying and relocating to live in a northwestern Ontario town.

Our family later moved closer to the centre of the town where they remained until my father returned from the war and they purchased the old farm in South Mindoka. My early memories of the farm life are vague at best. I am, however, able to recall a few occurrences, some quite humorous and some not quite so humorous, of those long ago times. One memory that stands out quite clearly in my memory, involved the purchase of a much needed team of working farm horses. Horses, during this era were a vital necessity for a subsistence farmer as they had not yet been fully replaced by the much more expensive to operate gasoline tractors.

 My father had apparently heard from a local man named Kirk Turner, who owned and operated a nearby Shell gasoline station, that another farmer in the Hough Lake area had a team of young, semi-broken horses for sale at quite a reasonable price, so he set out to see, and possibly, to purchase them for use on the farm. Kirk Turner, knowing the team's owner as well as the location of the owner's farm, accompanied my father and myself back to the horse owner's remotely located farm to see if he could make a deal with the owner and purchase the team. This farm was about three miles down a dirt road that was, at the time, impossible for Kirk's old pick-up truck so we were forced to leave the truck and walk the three miles back to the farm. As I was, at the time, only five years of age, I soon found it quite impossible to keep up with the long quick strides of my father and Kirk. I was soon left far behind, sobbing in frustration and struggling quite unsuccessfully to catch up to them. When I finally realized that I was not going to catch up to the two men who were by now far ahead of me, I yelled out to my father. "Wait for me, Daddy, wait up for me."

 My father continued on his way without even looking back or acknowledging my pleading cries. Kirk Turner, however, kept looking back in a very concerned manner at this crying little boy who, at that time, could not understand why his daddy did not care enough for him to stop and wait for a few moments for him to catch up. I could hear Kirk quite clearly suggesting to my father that they should stop and let me catch up to them.

My father, however, responded to these comments from Kirk by saying loudly, "Oh, don't worry about the kid, Kirk, he will be okay, we will find him on our way out if he can't keep up."

We were, at that point in time, about two miles back on this old farm access trail, and in the midst of a dark, gloomy forest that frightened me immensely, with my vivid young imagination making the situation appear much worse than reality ever could. This was probably about the first time in my young life that I began to understand and realize that my father did not care for or about me in any way or any manner, and that he also did not care if anyone else knew that fact. It was also the time when I began to realize that I could not rely on, or depend on my father for anything and that I had only myself to rely on and guide me through my childhood as I grew to manhood.

This was not to be the last time that my father was to display his total lack of interest or care of myself as you will read in future chapters. My father did, however purchase that team of young semi-broken horses on that long-ago day. He also, at the same time, purchased the appropriate harness for the team and then was forced to walk them the eight or so miles back to the farm while family friend Kirk took me home in his old pick-up.

This new team of young horses was just two years old and only barely broken to harness and were not in the least, familiar with any of the various implements such as plows, discs, harrows, stone boats and hay wagons used on and about the farm. The next six to eight months proved to be quite exciting and nearly always hilarious, especially to us children, and sometimes to our mother who would at times have difficulty concealing her amusement from our father. This amusement was caused by the new team of horses propensity to nearly always take wild flight each and every time that father would harness them to a new piece of farm equipment. Father, for some reason, found no amusement whatsoever in his young teams wild antics as he would often find himself being dragged across the open fields or across the fresh manure-covered barnyard by his rambunctious young, unbroken team as he attempted to stop its chaotic flight. Our father was probably quite fortunate that he was not killed or seriously injured by these semi-wild horses during this era as he was dragged, kicked and knocked over by them on many a occasion.

It was only after about six to eight months of severe whippings, beatings, curses, kicks, punches and other various abuses by our father that the team finally become complacent and accepting enough of its position of servitude on the farm and in the hierarchy of things to become a reasonably useful team of working farm horses.

I recall one humorous incident during haying season when mother came running home from the fields where she and Father had been loading the seasoned hay that had been stacked to dry in the fields onto the hay wagon in order to haul it back to where it would be stored in the old barn's big hayloft. Mother was quite excited and upset, as apparently, the semi-broken team had run off across the field dragging a full load of hay with Father bouncing along on the very top of the huge load as he attempted to stop the crazed run. Apparently the team only made it partway across the big field when the large steel-rimmed wheels of the hay wagon struck a small ridge, causing the wagon and its entire load of hay to flip over on top of our unfortunate, cursing father. Mother then rushed home to get me and Doreen to come with her to help get Father dug out from under the hay and to help get him home as she thought he was probably quite badly hurt. As we exited the house to go and rescue Father, we could see him leading the now subdued and badly-beaten young team of horses into the log barn where the two of them were to receive a further whipping for their disobedience. Apparently, the load of fresh hay had cushioned Father from any serious harm other than the many injuries and bruises to his pride.

Another mentionable incident relating to our father's cruel and insensitive nature occurred when I was about seven or eight years of age. This was the time in late fall, when one of the two young horses died for some unrecalled reason. Father, ever the opportunist, pulled, with the surviving horse, the dead animal back to the edge of the furthest-most farm field, cut him open and then spread cyanide or some other similar deadly poison all over and inside the freshly opened carcass. His plan was that some of the many wolves and foxes that, at that time, roamed around and through South Mindoka in the surrounding forests and on the old farm would, as winter came on and their food sources became scarce, partake of some of the easily obtainable and freshly poisoned horse meat and die on the spot. He would then skin the unfortunate animal and be able to claim the twenty-five dollar bounty that the Province had placed on each wolf killed. He also hoped to reap more money by selling the wolf and fox skins to a local trapper who would in turn sell them to a fur buyer. He never did manage to get any of the wolves or foxes but unfortunately our pet collie Lassie did. Lassie, who was very pregnant at the time was kept outside on the porch at night was quite free to roam about the farm.

Lassie was, to us children, a extraordinarily smart animal, a devoted friend and playmate to both Doreen and me. She was not only a ever ready playmate to us but she was also a hard working and extremely intelligent cattle dog. I can readily recall stepping out on the porch of the house on many occasions and simply saying to Lassie, "Lassie, go get the cows." That beautiful, faithful collie dog would, after hearing that command, head off into the fields and forests of the farm and, if necessary, the adjoining wilds. She would even, if necessary, swim across the river that flowed through our property. I cannot recall her ever returning to the farmhouse unless she had the entire herd of milk cows moving along in front of her to the barn. Even when the cattle escaped from our fenced off areas, Lassie would find them and bring them home.

One early winter evening, not long after the unfortunate dead horse had been placed out and seeded with the deadly poison, Doreen and I heard our precious, pregnant Lassie whimpering softly at the porch door. When we checked to see what the ruckus was all about, we found her lying on the porch deck, surrounded by her nine dead, freshly aborted little puppies, gasping and retching in the last few moments of her life. She died in our arms that cold winter night long ago, as we attempted, to no avail, to comfort her and ease her terrible pain. She had apparently found, and always hungry, consumed some of the poisoned horsemeat. Needless to say, when we called out to Father, asking what he could do for her, he just grunted and replied something like, "just let the fool animal die, she should have known better than to eat that damn horse meat".

Our beautiful pet Lassie, her unborn puppies, Doreen and myself were fortunately, the only known victims of our father's callous and careless use of wolf poison. There were, in all probability, many other victims that consumed the poisoned horsemeat and then dragged themselves off to die somewhere deep in the wilderness forests that comprised the majority of our farm.

Fortunately, our family did not know at that particular time, but our younger brother Don, not yet even born, was to very nearly be, many years later, another victim of our father's callous and careless use of this deadly poison.

While we were to have many more pet dogs on that old farm, the memories of our dear Lassie and her untimely death will always remain with us.

Chapter 3

The Rifle

During our father's four-year-long wartime absence, our Great-uncle Peter, a former Northern prospector and trapper, had resided with us in town while he worked in the local gold mines. Shortly before our father returned from the war, uncle Peter moved out of the family home and relocated to a small nearby town that was about twenty miles south of where we lived.

After we had moved to the Mindoka farm, I was not to see or hear from Uncle Peter again for about twelve years. In later years I was, and to this very day I am, puzzled by the total lack of any contact whatsoever by our uncle Peter following his sudden departure from the family home. As he had been like a father and quite close to me, Doreen and our mother, it appeared quite peculiar that neither side made or attempted to make any kind of contact with the other following Uncle Peter's departure. Whenever I asked my mother about Uncle Peter and why he never came to visit, she always managed to evade giving me any kind of positive reply. Given my knowledge now of my parents' wartime and pre-wartime activities, whatever it was that caused this lack of contact by Uncle Peter and our family would not surprise me.

* * *

Some twelve years later, I happened to be working on a highway construction project and was living with my mother's father and her stepmother who, at that time, were operating a gentleman's farm near a little town close to where Uncle Peter lived. While living there, I convinced my grandfather, to take me to see Great-uncle Peter who was his younger brother. I wanted to see my Uncle Peter again as I had nothing but good memories of him from my younger days when he lived with us. Grandfather for some unknown reason was quite reluctant at first but I finally convinced him to take me to see him as I did not know exactly where he lived. I did get to see my uncle again but he, for some unknown reason, seemed to act quite embarrassed and distant during the short visit. I could tell that I had made Uncle Peter quite uncomfortable with my unannounced visit to his home. The main and most important reason for my wishing to see him again was, however, to just thank him for a gift that he had presented me with, just prior to his leaving the family home those many years ago. This gift had been a little "Canuck" twenty-two caliber, single-shot rifle that he had carried with him for many years in the wilds of Northern Ontario and Quebec during his prospecting and trapping days. I had no way of knowing at the time he was presenting that little rifle to me, but that rifle was to become, in the future, a cherished possession of mine and would serve me well for many years, giving me a means of escape from a terribly rough abusive home life.

While I was never, in my younger years, permitted to take this little 22-caliber Canuck rifle out on my own, our Uncle Frank, who lived not far from us with his family in a even more remote area, would occasionally bring over a few twenty-two shells and supervise me in a little target practice in our back yard. As this was the only firearm the family possessed at that time, it was also used to shoot or frighten off the ever-present and persistent chicken hawks that preyed upon the farms poultry. It was also used by my father and our friend Ian Lott during their annual butchering of pigs and steers that the family raised and utilized for our winter's meats. As can be imagined, once I had become reasonably proficient in handling the little rifle, I was constantly harassing my parents, with no success whatsoever, to permit me, a just-turned nine-year-old boy, to take it out on my own to go grouse or rabbit hunting.

* * *

It was mid September; the multi-colored deciduous leaves had begun to drop, the scent of fall was in the air and on most mornings, the grass was covered with a thin white layer of frost. I was only nine and one half years of age when Father, after much pleading by me, suddenly took the rifle and a few shells out from the closet that was under the stairwell. Handing the rifle and shells to me, he finally said the words I had waited so long to hear. "Okay, let's go hunting."

When I finally realized that what I had been hoping for was now finally happening, we were already out, over the ravine and past the old log barn, walking along a muddy cow trail that paralleled a electrified barbed-wire fence that usually, but not always, kept the cattle and the horses within a reasonable distance. Father told me to load the little single shot weapon but to leave it un-cocked, so I did so, leading the way as I had been directed, with the rifle at the ready in eager anticipation of spotting some kind of shootable game, rabbit or partridge. We had only gone a short distance when I heard a clucking sound and observed a small clump of bushes just off the trail rustling and waving about as whatever was in it moved around, feeding or just scratching around in the forest floor's litter.

"That sounds like a partridge," I said to my bored father.

"Well then, don't just talk, go ahead and shoot it," he replied.

Cocking the little rifle, I took careful aim at the center of that clump of brush and pulled the trigger. Following the shot, we heard a sudden fluttering of wings and then total silence.

"I think I got him," I said.

"Well then, go pick him up so we can move along," said Father.

I handed him the rifle and went over to the clump of brush and pulled out my first ever victim of that little rifle, a large black and white woodpecker. With a stunned look of disbelief, I blurted out to Father, "It's just a woodpecker, it's not a partridge."

Father just handed back the rifle to me and said, "Yes it is, but you said it was a partridge before you shot and without your knowing what it really was; now let's go home, that's enough hunting for today."

Father said nothing more until we were nearly home when he said, "Don't you ever do that again, you must never shoot or even point a gun at anything unless you are positive that you know what it is and you are positive that you want to kill it. Now when we get home, don't tell your mother what you did as she would be really mad. You are to only take your rifle out by yourself and not when Danny is here."(Danny was a neighboring boy who lived about a mile from us who I frequently played with.)

I have always remembered this event with total clarity. This unusual display of genuine concerned behavior and benevolence towards me by my father was to be the first and the last time that I could recall him ever teaching or treating me like a son.

***

The little twenty-two single shot rifle was, over the following years, to put many a meal of rabbit or partridge on the family's dinner table during times that they would otherwise have gone hungry. With this little gun I also had a reason and the wherewithal to be able to escape from the angry, dysfunctional household that I was compelled to live in. I now had a reason as well as a trusty friend who I could depend on to protect me from real as well as imagined dangers as I explored the vast Mindoka wilderness. I was, over the following years, to spend many long days in every season of the year, roaming about the Mindoka forests in my mostly unsuccessful endeavors at escaping Father's wrath.

Chapter 4

Wolfskin

In nineteen forty-six, the Mindoka area was very sparsely populated with only a few subsistence farms scattered about. Wildlife in the area had begun to multiply and recover from the subsistence food hunting of the hungry thirties. As a result, there were plenty of wild whitetail deer and moose roaming about, feeding in the overgrown abandoned fields and willow-filled swamps that covered the lands. This abundance of wild game animals meant that the wild carnivores such as the red fox and the grey wolves of the North also grew in abundance.

In late fall about two years after our move to the South Mindoka farm, Father, with the assistance of an old family friend named Ian Lott, slaughtered one of the farm's steers for our winter's supply of meat. This procedure took place regularly, each and every fall and usually involved the death of a steer, one or two pigs and a multitude of chickens, ducks and geese. Normally the slaughtering process occurred after the onset of the cold weather came, ensuring that any fresh meat could be cut, wrapped and stored in the meat-shed where it would soon freeze solid and remain so preserved until consumed by our growing family. As the cold fall season gradually slipped into the long winter's icy grips, the outside temperature would rarely rise much above ten or fifteen degrees above zero. The colder winter months of January and February often brought forty degrees below zero temperatures and occasionally even fifty or sixty degrees below. A commonly heard night sound on the farm during the really cold weather was the loud, rifle-like cracks of the woodland poplar and birch trees as their trunks, freezing solid, exploded from the extreme cold.

    The killing, eviscerating, skinning and quartering of the unfortunate candidate that had been selected to become that winter's food for our family, normally took place just to the East of the old log barn that was located across a deep ravine to the North of the farm house. This was the favored site during the early years for the butchering procedure as there were tall sturdy trees that could be used to hang the unfortunate animal from after he or she had been summarily executed by a bullet in the brain fired from my little twenty-two single-shot rifle. This hanging from the trees made the bleeding, evisceration and skinning process much easier than if done with the dead animal lying on the ground. Following the execution, evisceration and skinning of the unfortunate animal, its remains were, as was the normal practice, disposed of by rolling them down and over the steep bank of the ravine where the local wild scavengers would soon make short work of them.

    It was only a very few days after one of these early year butchering events when the family began to hear their pet dog Lassie barking much more than was usual, late into the fall nights. She appeared quite agitated about something but what was even more unusual, she would not leave the protection of the covered porch to investigate whatever was bothering her and could not by any means be quieted. On about the fourth night of this persistent barking and growling, there was what farmers called, a harvest moon. This is a full moon that made the fall night sky and farm fields quite bright, especially since we also had at that particular time, about three inches of pure white snow covering the ground. On that bright cold night, long ago, when Doreen and I went out on the porch to see if we could see what was causing Lassie's anxiety. We could quite easily observe about five or six large grey timber wolves on the far bank of the ravine, tearing at the frozen remains of the recently butchered steer. We rushed back inside and had soon informed Father what we had seen.

He jumped up, uttered a few of his favorite profanities, grabbed my little twenty-two rifle and a few shells and went out on the porch after telling Doreen and myself to stay inside. After a moment or two, we heard the sharp crack of the twenty-two rifle as he fired. Father then left the porch and returned in about ten or so minutes, dragging a very large, very dead, three legged grey wolf behind him.

The next morning, with myself and Doreen watching closely, Father proceeded to skin out the wolf carcass. He then salted and nailed the pelt to the woodshed wall. Once it had dried and he had fleshed it thoroughly, he made patterns of his feet on pieces of cardboard, then transferred them to the wolf skin. Cutting out many different pieces of the wolf skin and making long leather lacing from the scraps, he had soon fashioned himself a pair of wolf skin moccasins that he wore proudly as slippers around the home for many years.

With the exception of a few additional eerie nighttime howling sessions and the occasional track on winter snows, we never again heard or saw any sign of the remaining wolves.

Chapter 5

Mathew - A Friend and Mentor

Soon after our family moved to their South Mindoka farm, Father decided that in addition to mixed farming, that he was going to become a logger and sawmill operator. This decision was prompted by the plentiful, mature, valuable timber growing on the large forested areas of the property. The fact that spruce and pine logs and lumber were in high demand in the south and were bringing good prices probably played a major role in his decision to log the farm's forests. The fact that we were always short of cash during those early years probably had a major influence on him to log the woodlands. In addition a local forestry contractor agreed to supply Father with logs if he was to set up a small sawmill on our property. It also kept him busy during the long cold winter months when farm work, due to the extreme cold, was at its "quietest time".

As these ventures, combined with farming, were just too much for one person to handle alone, Doreen and myself, at nine and seven years of age had our daily workloads substantially increased. Once the logging and sawmill ventures were begun Doreen was assigned the milkmaid position and had to milk the three cows twice daily. My tasks were to ensure the cattle were secure in their stalls and properly watered with hand-pumped water that I had to carry in large buckets up the hill from the well after filling them. I also had to ensure that they were fed with hay that had to be first, forked down from the barns hay loft and then carried with a pitchfork to the individual cattle stalls. I then had to ensure that any fresh manure was hand-shoveled out of the barn and onto the big manure pile located just a few feet away from the big double barn doors. All this work was preceded by us first having to find the cattle from wherever they had strayed on the farm and then bring them back to the barn and their individual stalls for milking. We were then required to carry the raw milk, in pails, across the deep ravine to the house where we used a hand-turned cream separator that operated by centrifugal force to separate the thick rich cream from the milk. We then carried the cream and milk down the steep hill to the big storage cans that were kept immersed in the cool little creek that bubbled along the ravines bottom as it awaited the creamery trucks twice weekly arrival from the Town of Englehart. We did retain sufficient milk and cream to provide the family with milk, fresh hand-churned butter and the rich thick buttermilk that was enjoyed by both Doreen and I.

In addition to Doreen's and my many forced contributions to the farm labors, once the logging of the farm lands began, Father decided that he needed to hire a worker to assist him in his entrepreneurial ventures in the fields of logging and sawmill work. A middle aged man of Finnish ancestry lived nearby and had frequently came to the farmhouse door seeking work of any kind. This man, Matthew Dawson, had assisted the family in the earlier home enlargement project soon after the family's arrival on the farm. Father made the decision to hire Mathew to assist him as he had already proven himself to be a very versatile and reasonably dependable worker. He lived in the local area and he worked for little money. Mathew was a small thin wizened, chain smoker of roll-your-own cigarettes, whose appearance always reminded me and Doreen of the comic strip character, 'Popeye the Sailor Man'.

Mathew was also full of valuable information about all sorts of things that were of vital interest to a young farm boy who had no money but plenty of raw materials, tools and ambition. Things like the location of nearby fishing holes, how to fashion a whistle out of an early spring willow twig, how to snare the wild snowshoe rabbits, how to manufacture a bow and arrow, how to make a moose call out of a piece of birch bark, etc. etc. With very little coaxing he would sit down and after rolling himself a cigarette, relate stories about the area's history, of its residents and of his own interesting past. He told we two children of how his people, the Finnish population living in the area would hunt deer using only homemade spruce skis and a sharp knife. They would chase the deer down on their skis in the deep snow and when the deer tired, ski up along-side them and cut their throats. A longtime bachelor, Mathew lived by himself in a small wood-frame cabin about two miles from our homestead. He had electric power in his cabin, supplied by a wind-powered wooden propeller that he had attached to a car generator, all mounted on a wooden tower and all built by himself. He had a indoor flush toilet that was operated by water that he hand-pumped into a barrel that he mounted in his cabin's rafters, gravity feeding his toilet's flush mechanism. He was one of the most interesting people that any young rural living boy could have ever met. He would often just show up at the farmhouse door at, or just before mealtimes as he knew that Mother would always welcome him in to eat whatever we had to offer. He was always ever tolerant of Mr. Marlowe's cynical put-down remarks about him "sponging" from the family and he would usually remain until late evening, chain smoking his handmade cigarettes and relating to we two children entertaining stories of his past.

 Father, with Mathew's assistance, soon had a thriving logging and sawmill operation under way. A nearby logging company also contributed immensely to their workload and profits by provided them with extra saw logs for custom contract sawing. These logs were in addition to the logs that Father and Mathew cut in the three-hundred and sixty acre forested farm that we owned. This forest logging was done mainly during the cold winter months using long two-person steel crosscut saws and the logging horse, Barney. Mother would also often travel back into the woods and assist Father in this difficult and dangerous logging operation, handling one end of the long crosscut saw whenever Mathew failed to show up for work. I can also recall watching Mr. Marlowe and Mathew, before Father purchased the sawmill, hand hewing with a heavy broad-axe valuable railroad ties out of the big spruce logs; railroad ties that the local Ontario Northland railway was always in the market for. Father eventually purchased a Massey-Harris rubber-tired tractor that served many purposes on the farm. This tractor was only purchased by Father after nearly a year of his unsuccessful attempts with Mathew at refurbishing an old dodge engine that he thought he could use to power his new sawmill. The tractor was to be used to power the sawmill, to haul the logs out from the forest to the mill, to pull the farm equipment and even as a delivery vehicle to fetch groceries and mail from the Post Office in Earlton to the home as the family at this time did not own any other means of transportation.

Although Mother never learned to drive a car, she seemed to enjoy driving that Massey-Harris tractor. She used it for transportation everywhere, including going to the local general store and Post Office. She would always drive it at full speed (about thirty miles per hour) wherever she went and regardless of road conditions with the groceries beside or behind her. On the few occasions that I was obliged to ride with her, I was forced to stand on the tractor's tow bar and hold on for dear life to the driver's metal seat that Mother was sitting on. I usually ended up in a stunned or terrified state as Mom seemed to know only one speed: full speed ahead. Straightaway, hill or around a curve, it did not matter, the only speed she knew was high gear with the throttle in a wide open position. Even now, years later I can still remember, and often relate the story of one terrifying ride down the steep hill to the Blanche River Bridge just below our farm. I swear that Mother took one sharp corner so fast going down that steep hill that the tractor went up on two wheels, scaring me so badly, that I jumped off my precarious perch on the back of the tractor, skinning my hands and knees quite badly on the rough gravel roadway. Mother never did seem able to understand or at least acknowledge that the tractor could operate quite well in a lower gear or at a slower speed. I often said in later years that I actually thought that she may have had some maniacal tendencies because when I would scream at her to slow down, she would just laugh and yell at me, "Hang on, Bobby, hang on!"

One winter, Mr. Marlowe and Mathew decided that, rather than walk or ski the long distance through the deep snow banks and the forest to the chosen logging area each and every day, it would be better to build a cabin within the logging area for Mathew to live in while he was logging. Mathew, using the areas big logs and the horse Barney, soon had a small sturdy log cabin erected in the midst of the choicest logging area. For heat and cooking he made up a round barrel stove with a flat steel top, four steel legs and a steel-hinged door bolted on to it. This stove, when properly stoked up with dry pine, spruce or alder, would get cherry red in no time flat, heating that little cabin so well that even on the coldest of days Mathew was forced to leave the cabin's door ajar. Mathew was to spend two full winters in that little cabin in the wild, cutting and piling saw logs for the mill. I would, on nearly every weekend, or at every available opportunity, if not at school or cutting firewood, put on my homemade skis, grab my trusty little rifle and sometimes a loaf of Mother's homemade bread or a jar of home-canned fruit, and ski off to see if Mathew was okay. I would also, if the opportunity presented itself, shoot Mathew a rabbit or partridge while on my way back to see him. Mathew was always really glad to see me and would stop working to go back to his little cabin, make a pot of tea and share whatever food he had available with me. As we drank and ate Mathew would tell me about the past weeks happenings and then take me out and show me what logging area he had worked in and what he had accomplished since my last visit.

He had also built a log lean-to up against the cabin for the farm horse that the family had, named Barney. Barney was used to skid the felled and limbed logs over the snow and frozen ground to a central log pile at the edge of one of the logging roads that Mathew was also required to build through the cutting areas to await hauling out to the mill site in early spring prior to the grounds thawing out. I always enjoyed watching this pair of old loggers working together as Barney seemed to know just exactly what to do and when to do it. With very few verbal commands from Mathew he would, once hitched to a log, just sort of hunker down and give a sharp tug to first, break the log free from the frozen earth and get it moving on the snow and then he would, on his own, with no further directions or commands from Mathew, tow it out of the bush where it had fallen to the log pile where he would stop and wait for Mathew to catch up and unhook him from the log or make some further minor adjustment to the logs position before unhooking him so they could go back for the next log or logs. I really enjoyed watching Barney on those long ago cold winters days, dragging his reins on the snow with a log behind him. When he arrived at the log pile he would stop, turn his head to look back at Mathew as if to say to him, "Will you hurry up and unhook me so I can go back and get the next log ?"

* * *

Father's ventures into the mixed farming and logging businesses were only to last about five years. An injury caused by a explosion during his war service in Italy brought about severe rheumatoid arthritis that was to soon totally ravage his entire body leaving him in severe and constant pain that would frequently send him off to the Military hospital in Toronto. His illness prevented him from performing any further farm or forest work whatsoever. He eventually sold off all the farm animals with the exception of the horse Barney who he never did use again but still, for some reason, kept for a few more years. He also sold off all the farming and logging equipment and then, to my chagrin, eventually sold all the remaining standing timber on the farm property to another local logging firm who soon stripped our lands of all the remaining timber of worth.

Mathew continued to visit us on occasion, continuing to perform odd jobs around the farm such as using an old homemade autotrac to haul our next year's supply of firewood out of the woods to the farmhouse. This autotrac was home-made from a old Ford car that had the body removed and the back wheels replaced with huge steel-cleated iron wheels about five feet in diameter. These huge drive wheels were turned by small gears on the vehicle's rear axle that meshed with the big gears that were welded to the inside of the big drive wheels' iron rims. This big homemade tractor was quite powerful but was really slow and rough to ride on, especially on pavement where the big steel cleats would clunk and clank as they struck the hard surface of the asphalt. These types of tractors were eventually banned from paved roads as they could easily damage the asphalt.

* * *

I also recall a humorous event one cold Christmas Eve many years past concerning Mathew that very nearly ended in tragedy and his demise. This occurred during one of the years that Mathew was living in his log cabin deep in the forests of our property as he logged the thick forests. Mother had invited him to come to supper in our home on this long ago Christmas Eve. Mathew appeared early with a bottle of whiskey for

Father and himself to drink in their celebration of the Yule time season. Mathew proceeded to get quite intoxicated so Mother attempted, to no avail, to convince him to stay and spend the cold night on our living room sofa. Mathew bravely declined this offer, stating that he could easily walk the mile or so through the deep snows to his remote log cabin located deep in our forest. It was quite late and very dark when Mathew left for his long walk that cold night. Approximately an hour following his departure, we were all awakened by our dog's loud barking from the porch where he spent the nights. Turning the porch light on, I could see where the deep snow on the trail leading down the hill and up to the fields and the path that led to Mathews cabin had been packed down to about a ten foot width on either side where Mathew had fallen and rolled down the hill. He, apparently had then gotten up to climb the hill again and again, only to fall and roll again to the bottom. It appeared that he must have repeatedly fallen and climbed both sides of the hill as the trail was hard packed on both sides. Returning to the warmth of our house I quickly dressed and followed the wide trail down the hill to where I found Mathew, lying and nearly frozen but sound asleep in the cold winter snow. Rousing him, I dragged him up the hill and into the house where I removed his outer snow-covered clothes and lay him on the sofa beside the warm wood heater. Totally embarrassed, Mathew was up and gone before any of the family the next morning. Neither he nor I ever spoke of this nearly tragic yet somewhat humorous incident again.

 Mathew's visits to the our home gradually decreased over the years and finally stopped altogether as Father's disparaging and often demeaning remarks finally had the desired effect on him. I continued, however, to frequently visit and assist the now-aging Mathew at his home for many more years. At one visit to Mathew's home, on a cloudy day with intermittent showers, Mathew asked me to assist him in removing his wind-powered generator from its tall wooden tower so that he could make some much needed repairs to it. Once I had climbed up and retrieved the generator from the tower, Mathew, ever the friendly sort, asked me to come into his two room house for a cup of tea. As we were sitting there in the kitchen, sipping away, (Mathew always drank his hot tea from the saucer after pouring it there from his cup to cool it down) a bolt of lightning suddenly flashed and struck the tower that I had just climbed down from. The bolt of lightning then travelled down the wires that connected the tower to Mathew's house and flashed out of the ceiling light fixture. After blowing the fixture to pieces it arced across the room to strike and blow up a oil lantern that was hanging from the wall. The oil lantern exploded and splattered the two of us with oil as we sat in stunned amazement. A really close call!

Mathew passed away peacefully, in his own bed in his own little home in nineteen sixty-five and was buried in a small Finnish cemetery in Marquis Township in Northern Ontario. I still think of Mathew with much fondness and still, after some fifty years, miss this kind, generous little man. Mathew was a good man, a good friend, a confidant and good counselor to a very sad and unhappy young boy who was living a very troubled childhood. I still miss you Mathew, wherever you are. I also still remember the time you gave me that little pearl-handled penknife of yours that I liked so much - my first knife. Thank you, Mathew, my friend. I think of you well, I think of you kindly and often.

Chapter 6

Farming

In addition to the two semi-tame horses that Father had purchased, we also had on our farm in the early years, three milking cows, usually from one to three calves that were produced by the cows each spring, a mean-tempered bull, three or four pigs, up to one hundred and fifty laying chickens of various ancestry, eight or ten geese, six or eight ducks, at least one dog, one or more cats, quite a few little kittens and at times, one or two caged pet birds, We also normally had large vegetable gardens, a huge potato patch and about twenty acres of hayfields. Our family was also fortunate to have, on our farm, copious quantities of wild strawberries, wild blueberries, wild raspberries, chokecherries, pincherries and delicious wild morel mushrooms. In addition, the lands also held many snowshoe hares, plenty of ruffed grouse, a few whitetail deer, many moose and many black bears as well as beaver, otter, lynx and other wild fur-bearers. A muddy river, the Blanche, also ran through the farm.

During the years that Father was involved in the logging and sawmill operations, the care, maintenance and operation of the farming operations was left primarily to Mother, Doreen and myself. Father's only involvement, as I recalled, was in the plowing, preparation and haying of the fields as well as the butchering each fall for the families food, a beef, a pig and many of the various fowl. Doreen's and my daily routines during this time period normally went something like this: we would get up from bed about six am, get the kitchen's wood-fired old cook-stove going, stoke up or restart the living room's wood heater (if the weather deemed it necessary) and get the kettle boiling on the kitchen stove so we could make Father's morning tea. After making Father's morning tea, we would deliver the first of usually two cups to him in his bedroom and then empty his bedside pot that was usually full of urine as Father found it much easier to urinate in a pot while in his bed rather than to get up to go to the bathroom.

Mother would then rise and prepare our breakfast of boiled oatmeal while we proceeded to the barn where Doreen would do the milking of the cows as I cleaned out the stable's manure and then fed and watered the cattle with water that I had to carry in pails from the well located just down the hill from the barn. I also had to slop (feed) and water the pigs and horses.

Once all this stable work was completed, we would put the cows and horses out to pasture and then carry the pails of milk back across the ravine to the house. After finally getting to eat our breakfast we would feed and water the poultry and collect the eggs. Our next chore was to separate the cream from the milk using a hand-cranked separator. I would then carry the separated cream and milk back down the ravine to the spring-fed creek where it was kept immersed in the cool, wood-encased pond that Father had built. This was used to keep the cream and milk cool until it was collected by the milk truck that came from the village of Englehart dairy twice weekly. If it was springtime and young calves were present on the farm, they would have to be then fed the separated raw milk from a pail. This calf feeding was required as it was necessary to wean the young animals as soon as possible after birth so that their mothers could again begin to give sellable milk.

If at any time butter was needed by our growing family, we would have to assist in the hand-churning of the cream until it formed itself into butter. This butter-making was enjoyed by me and Doreen as we usually got to drink some of the fresh, lumpy and delicious buttermilk that resulted from the butter making process.

Once all our morning chores were finished, we would then have to go and clean out the pigpens and the chicken house. My next daily task would normally be to chop sufficient fire-starting kindling for the farmhouse's wood heater and wood cook-stove and carry that day's supply of kindling along with the day's firewood requirements from the woodshed into the house.

Following the mornings routine workload we would go into the house where Mother would home-school us as there were no public schools within a reasonable distance. The closest school at that time was a little old one-room school that was located about five miles away, across the un-bridged muddy Blanche River. The Blanche River crossing of that time consisted of a small wooden raft and a long clothesline-like contraption that spanned the river about five feet above the water's level. The raft itself was permanently connected to the lower clothesline cable through another piece of wire cable. A river crossing was made by standing on the raft and simply reeling oneself across the river by pulling on the clothesline cable that then pulled the raft by the connecting cable to the opposite bank. If the raft was on the other side of the river, you stood on the bank and reeled it over to your side of the river with the same clothesline. This contraption only worked reasonably well during the summer days when the river was not too high from the spring thaws or heavy rains. During the fall and winter months crossings could only be made after the river ice had thickened sufficiently. It was much too far to travel and much too dangerous a river crossing for children as young as Doreen and I to attempt on our own. We would usually complete our home-schooling by about two in the afternoon, after which we would have the remainder of the afternoon free to work in the farm garden, pick wild berries for our mother to preserve or make into jams and jellies or do any of the numerous other farm chores. After this work was completed, we would begin again with the evening's milking and feeding of the animals. These evening chores were usually a fun time for me and Doreen as it normally began with us taking our pet dog Lassie to go out on the farm fields or into the forests to find and retrieve the wandering cattle so they could be stabled for the night and then fed, watered and milked. Doreen and I were, on more than one occasion as we brought home the cattle, "treed" by the farm's bad-tempered big bull that did not seem to appreciate being chased wildly through the woods and across the meadows by two carefree young children and one happy-go-lucky collie dog. Lassie would always attempt to chase the evil-tempered bull away from us but, once aroused, the bull was more than a match for the dog and would simply ignore her or sometimes even charge and chase after her.

Another chore that we had to assist in was the annual hay harvesting. Once the field hay of timothy, vetch and clover had been cut down, dried and raked into long windrows by Father using at first, our semi-wild team of horses and then later, the tractor, it became our responsibility to use a three-tined metal pitchfork to "stook" the hay into piles around the field that would permit it to properly dry out and season before it was collected and stored in the old log barns hayloft. If not properly dried and seasoned in this manner, the hay would, once stored in the barn loft, soon become moldy and be useless as winter food for the livestock.

* * *

A Father's Son

I can recall a incident that occurred when Doreen and I were given the responsibility of spreading and packing, with our small young feet, the loose hay that Father and Mother were throwing off the horse-drawn haywagon and up into the hayloft after it had been collected from the fields. As Doreen was only about eight or nine and I was about six or seven years of age, we were soon physically unable to keep pace with our adult parents and the loose dry hay began to pile up in the loft's doorway. In his attempt to speed his toiling young children up, Father began to curse us loudly and at length in an attempt to frighten us into working harder. Unsuccessful in this profanity method, he finally, in his frustration at our slowness, threw his steel-tined pitchfork at me, driving it firmly into my shin until the hardened steel tines finally hit, and were stopped by my shin bone.

* * *

Another similar memorable incident recalled was the time I, at about eight or nine years of age, accidentally slipped on the haywagon while spreading the loose hay that Father had thrown on the wagon from the fields. When my right foot suddenly slipped through the loose, widely-spaced boards of the hay wagon, it struck the top of one of the large steel-rimmed wagon wheels, driving my leg up so that it struck the bottom of my jaw, knocking me completely unconscious. I came to after only a moment or two to find myself flat on my back on the hay wagon with Father standing nearby, leaning on his pitchfork and laughing uproariously at the sight of his young son lying unconscious before him. As I recall, Father's only other reaction was to tell me to, "Get up off your damn back and get back to work." On another occasion I can recall received a vicious kick on my shin from one of Father's steel-toed logging boot for some unrecalled infraction that he had taken offence to and felt the need to severely punish me. Needless to say, by this time in my life, I had already reached the conclusion that for some unknown reason, my father really did not like me and that I should make every possible effort to avoid angering him and receiving a severe beating.

I was to soon discover that no matter what I did or attempted to do, that I would receive no advice, help or compliments from Father. I also was soon to discover that it mattered not how well I did something, Father was to always able to find fault with my performance. As I was to learn later in my life, Father had decided that I was not his birth son. As a result he was to express his anger and disappointment at my mother's supposed infidelity during his wartime absence by physically and mentally abusing both myself and Mother whenever the opportunity presented itself. At the time all this abuse was occurring, I could not know or understand why it was that it was I who always received the beatings and abuse, even though sister Doreen or possibly no-one may have been responsible for whatever had provoked Father into another beating.

Mother, however, knew what it was that drove her husband to both physically and mentally abuse his son, and occasionally, as he was beating me, she would beat the hapless Doreen in an always futile attempt to make him stop. This technique of hers never ever seemed to work on Father. Rightly or wrongly, Mother must have hoped that her simultaneous beating of Doreen as Father was wrongly beating me would make him see the error of his ways. Unfortunately for both me and Doreen, it never ever seemed to work that way.

In the evening once all of Doreen's and my farm chores were completed and it was dark, the family would huddle about our battery-powered radio listening to our favorite "Boston Blackie" or "The Green Hornet" radio serials. If nothing on the radio was of interest, Mother would light a coal-oil lamp and the family would sit about the dimly-lit room reading whatever was available. If the family had company or it was some special occasion, Father would get the big Coleman oil lamp out and light it. This lamp, with its pressurized oil fuel, emitted a much brighter light than the regular oil-wick type lamps. Its downside was that the special wick burnt out quite quickly and was quite expensive to purchase. I also read countless pocket books, usually Western or Mike Hammer novels, that friends and neighbors would give to us.

Doreen and I were usually permitted some time to themselves on weekends and some evenings that would enable us to play or to pursue our hobbies. This "time off," so to speak, was of course, completely dependent on the time of year. If it was springtime, we would be sent out to pick the wild mushrooms known as morels or the tiny, but plentiful, wild strawberries that Mother would soon make into the delicious wild strawberry jams that we would enjoy on homemade toasted bread during the long winter months. If it was mid-summer, we would be sent to picking the wild raspberries or wild blueberries that were also made into jams or were preserved in sweetened syrup in quart jars for later consumption as a desert by the growing farm family. In fall there was the tiny pincherries and chokecherries that made the most wonderful jellies, but were to be found, in that area, only by the steel bridge that was eventually constructed to cross the river that ran through and to the east of the farm. In later years Doreen and I could well recall the seemingly, hundreds of jars of jams, jellies, preserves and other farm and garden supplies stored in the dirt dugout cellar beneath the house awaiting their use during the long cold winter months. Each fall, our family would also preserve, in large ceramic crocks, hundreds of chicken eggs in a jelly-like substance called 'waterglass'. The waterglass apparently prevented the air from getting into the eggs causing them to spoil. In addition to Mother's preserving of the wild fruits and berries found on the farm, Father would, each fall, once the cold weather had set in, begin butchering the farm birds and animals for the family's winters consumption. He was usually assisted, for a share of the meat, by an old family friend, Ian Lott, who at that time still lived in New Liskeard, about sixteen miles from the farm. Ian would usually be accompanied by his wife Barb, their son Patrick and their daughter Mary and later by another son Jon and another daughter Cheryl. Father and Ian would spend the day slaughtering and butchering a beef or a pig or some of the numerous chickens, geese or ducks that our family had raised.

This annual butchering of the farm animals was usually quite traumatic for Doreen and I as we usually befriended at least some of these animals during their brief lives. We now had to observe these "almost family members" being killed, sometimes in a cruel or unorthodox method. What always made this butchering event even worse for us to witness was the fact that Father always seemed to be eager to attempt some "new and better way" to end the unfortunate animal or bird's existance on earth. In one instance Father and Mr. Lott took the condemned pig behind the old log barn that lay just across the ravine to the north of the house and instead of first shooting it in its brain with my little 22 rifle as was the usual means of execution, decided that it would bleed out much better if they simply slashed its throat with a sharp knife and then turned it loose to run about the barn yard until it had fully bled out and died. Unfortunately for the poor pig, (and for those of our family watching from a distance) the pig escaped their clutches before the throat slashing was fully completed. The first indication that the observers had that the procedure had gone wrong was the terrible squealing from the injured pig and the loud yelling and cursing coming from Father and Mr. Lott. The next thing the family observed was the poor pig, racing about the barnyard at top speed on the newly fallen snow with his life's blood spraying out of his partially cut throat, closely followed by two blood covered, would-be amateur butchers. On another pig-butchering event, they simply strung the unfortunate animal up by the severed tendons of his back legs and then, again without further ado, severed its juggler vein and watched it bleed out until it finally expired. This particular butchering event was to prove quite traumatic to me as I awoke during the following night, according to mother, screaming at the top of my lungs, "Don't cut my throat, please don't cut my throat!". While I cannot recall any of the details it is not to difficult to imagine what I must have been dreaming of that long ago night.

The chickens and other farm fowl were usually beheaded with a axe until again, Father decided to try out the "new improved method" of killing chickens that he had read about in some of the farm literature that we regularly received from some Government agency. This new method involved using a specially designed killing knife that the person doing the killing inserted into the bird's mouth and then twisted upwards so that the point of the knife punctured the bird's brain, supposedly killing it instantly. This new method worked quite well for Father most of the time, unless, as happened in many cases, Father missed the bird's brain with the knife, in which situation Doreen and I ended up chasing the poor wounded chicken around the yard to capture it, and return it to Father so he could finish the job properly.

* * *

The farm's big potato patch also provided Doreen and me with many long days of both welcome and unwelcomed entertainment. Father seemed to think that the plowing of about two acres of unbroken soil for the potato patch would be a great method of taming his two young semi-broken horses. We children found it quite hilarious to see those two horses running off across the field with that single-furrow steel plough bouncing along behind them and Father running close behind, cursing and yelling at the horses, "Whoa, you SOB's, whoa!" Unfortunately for us children, once the ground was finally plowed, disked and harrowed to our father's satisfaction, it became Doreen's and my task to mark out the rows, cut up the eyed seed potatoes, and then plant and cover them with the freshly-tilled soil. It was also our job, once the potatoes began growing, to walk along the rows of growing potatoes in the hot humid summer and hill up each plant with soil until they ceased growing and had blossomed. We then had to go out about every third day with a old tobacco can that was filled about half-full with kerosene, and with our fingers, pick the ever present and numerous potato bugs from the plant leaves that these pesky beetle-like insects liked to consume. We would then drop the potato bugs into the can where the kerosene would soon kill them. Once the potatoes had matured and the tops had frozen, we then had to hand dig all of these potatoes out of the ground, leave them on the surface of the ground to dry for a few days and then bag them. We then had to carry the heavy burlap bags of potatoes across the fields and ravine to the dugout root cellar under the house where they were stored in a large wooden box and covered with dried sawdust from the family sawmill.

Father's logging and sawmill enterprises came to an end soon after he was stricken with rheumatoid arthritis. He would spend months at a time in Toronto's Sunnybrook Veterans' Hospital undergoing treatment for his ever-worsening affliction. He eventually simply "gave up" and would spend the majority, if not all, of the day, in bed or sitting in the living room by the heater drinking hot tea, smoking roll-your-own cigarettes and urinating in a pot that Doreen or myself would have to empty and clean for him. This chore was not an easy one as the farm had no running water or electricity in the home for the first four or five years. We had no indoor plumbing whatsoever for the first few years and never did get a telephone. The only luxury in our home was a battery-powered radio that of course relied on a large expensive dry-cell battery that our family could rarely afford to purchase.

A Father's Son

* * *

When I was about nine years of age, Father finally had our old friend, Mathew Dawson drill, with a hand auger, a potable-water well directly under the home's kitchen sink through a hole they cut in the floor for that purpose. Fortunately, Mathew hit water at about twenty feet so they then installed a hand-operated lever pump to bring the water up to the kitchen. The kitchen sink was drained down and out through a pipe installed in a trench about six feet deep and about one-hundred and fifty feet long that went over the bank and into the ravine that separated the house from the old barn. I can still easily remember the details of, and thelabor that was involved in the digging of this trench quite clearly as I was the nine-year-old boy who had to hand dig it, down at least six feet deep in the iron-hard clay. This depth was required so that it would drain properly and be well below the frost line so as to not freeze during the long cold winter months. I first had to dig and chop through the hard surface red clay with a pick and shovel, shovel the dirt up and away from the trench, install the drain pipe in the trench and then cover it over with the excavated material. I really did not mind this work as it meant that once completed I would no longer have to carry the buckets of household waste water from under the kitchen sink where it was kept to catch the dirty water from the sink drain. The newly drilled well and the hand-operated pump meant that I also no longer had to carry fresh water to the house from the old wood-encased well that was located at the bottom of the steep ravine just north of the house.

At about this same time period, the family finally graduated from having to use the old wood-frame outhouse to having an "indoor toilet." Anyone who has ever had the pleasure of sitting on a frost-covered rural outhouse seat in minus forty degree weather will recognize just how the family appreciated this upgrading of their "bathroom facilities." Our parents even replaced (at least some of the time) the shiny-paged Simpson's or Eaton's catalogues with genuine toilet paper when their finances permitted!. Of course, these "improvements" also added to my personal workload as I now had to carry the five-gallon toilet pail full of human waste out of the house and dump it downthe old outhouse pit that was located about seventy-five feet from the house. With two adults and eventually six children in the household, this "emptying of the honey bucket" usually had to be done on a daily basis.

As Father's illness progressed he gradually sold off (or the family consumed) all of the remaining farm animals. This course of action was necessitated by the lack of available money for animal and bird feed and Father's inability to work in order to earn that much needed asset. He did retain, for some forgotten reason, one of his horses for a few more years before finally selling him as well. Doreen and I were, by now, attending a regular public school in Kirkland Lake and as a result we had to leave the family home quite early in the morning and did not return until quite late. We could no longer, therefore properly look after the farm animals or cope with all the work that was required to operate a farm. The farm eventually had no cattle, pigs, horses, chickens or any other domestic animals or birds left and only a large vegetable garden raked out of the hard, infertile clay of Northern Ontario. Doreen and I also had to tend this garden during the spring and summer months. This vegetable garden, with its multitudes of fast-growing weeds and poor production kept me and Doreen quite busy pulling and hoeing amidst the hordes of mosquitoes, black flies, horse flies, deer flies and "no-see-ums." The purchasing and use of commercial fertilizers was, due to the lack of money, never a viable option for our money-poor family. We did utilize, as much as possible, as fertilizer, the old rotted manure from the pile in front of the barn where it had been piled and composted. Once all these changes on the farm had taken place, my workload changed considerably. I was now also delegated the task of providing wood fuel for the homes cast iron wood heater and kitchen cook-stove. As our family was at this time, completely dependent on wood fuel for cooking and heating, the chore of cutting down the trees and then getting this fuel to the home and to the state where it could be used was essential. The task of firewood cuttingentailed heading off with a four foot 'swedesaw' and axe out to the woodcutting area that was usually about one-half mile or more from the farmhouse. As the woodcutting chore was normally done during the colder winter months, I would have Mother make me a sandwich and a thermos of hot tea to take with me for my lunch. I would then take off on my homemade cross-country skis for the day. A year's supply of firewood usually consisted of about eight to ten four foot cords of pine, birch and poplar wood that I would cut, split and place in strategically-located piles where they would be left until early spring when Mathew, using his old homemade autotrac and wagon, would, with my assistance, haul it out over the rough forest roads that I had also cleared during the long cold winter months so as to provide easy passage. We would stack the wood in the farm yard near the big woodshed to further dry out in the summer heat. This woodcutting task, although hard work, was not completely unwelcomed as it permitted myself a means and a excuse to escape from the frustration, arguments, fights, beatings and putdowns that seemed to be daily events and quite normal for our household.

After the firewood had been brought to the house, stacked and further dried, I would then have to cut all this wood into twelve to fourteen inch stove-box lengths with the four foot swedesaw. I then had to, with a four pound axe, split and again pile this wood, leaving it to air dry even more until it was reasonably seasoned and would readily burn in the home's cook-stove and living room heater. Once dried to Father's satisfaction I would then carry it and pile it in the woodshed to further dry and await it's use during the following year. The next chore involving the firewood was to, nearly each and every day of the year, cut some of the driest wood into the smaller kindling that was used along with paper to start the heating and cooking fires each and every morning, winter or summer. I then had to carry this kindling and sufficient wood into the house for use that day. A normal day's use would consist of a armload of kindling and four to six armloads of firewood. Eventually, the family was to replace the old wood heater in their living room as the main source of heat with a more convenient oil space heater that I then had to keep fueled with kerosene. This kerosene, or coal oil as it was called, was purchased in bulk and stored in a shed in forty-five-gallon drums. My job was to tap off, into one-gallon glass jars, three or four gallons of this oil each and every day to replenish the oil stove's reservoir.

* * *

When I was about eleven or twelve years of age, our grandmother on Mother's side, with whom Mother had finally reconciled after many years of absolutely no contact whatsoever, came to visit us. Grandmother Lenora Armstrong and her pimp boyfriend Arnold, had, apparently, or so us children had been told, kidnapped Mother when she was quite young, from her natural father who had at that time legal custody of her, and run off to the USA, to work there as a prostitute. The natural grandfather finally located her and went down across the U.S. border to "rescue" his daughter, our mother, taking her back, and raising her in Canada. The grandmother eventually returned to Canada with her "pimp" boyfriend where they lived together as man and wife in various Ontario locations until her death. When the visiting grandmother and her common-law husband observed the conditions that our family was living in on our Mindoka farm, she immediately gave our destitute family enough money to purchase an electric water pump, (by now we did have basic electricity in the house) a flush toilet and a proper bathtub for bathing. Again, and unfortunately for me, I was elected at eleven years of age to be, under Fathers strict supervision, the laborer and installer of all these new modern conveniences. This job entailed the digging, again by hand and in the iron-hard clay of our yard, all of the required trenches and the big pit for a septic tank and the drainage fields. I also had to dig a new six foot deep trench from the house, across the yard and down the hill to the much larger, fourteen foot deep, four foot diameter well that I was also required to dig by hand. I dug this new well near the old reliable wood-enclosed spring-fed well that had replaced the one just below the barn. Father had decided a few years earlier to have Mathew dig this new well near the cold, spring-fed pool that was at the bottom of the hill adjoining the farmhouse. I was also to install, by myself, a four foot diameter galvanized steel casing in this very productive well that is probably still in use today. Again, I did not overly mind all of this hard work as the newly-installed flush toilet and electric water pump meant that I no longer had to carry that five-gallon toilet pail full of human waste out to the outdoor toilet each and every day; summer and winter.

Grandmother Armstrong and her common-law husband, eventually were to construct an addition onto the east end of our farm home and reside with our family for a few years. Eventually the severe winters of Northern Ontario and the remote location of our home caused them to relocate to the Lake Simcoe area of Southern Ontario where they remained and lived until their demise many years later.

Although Father always seemed to be much too ill to perform any of the routine household chores or to do any yard or farm work of any kind, he always seemed ever capable and more than willing to produce more children. When he and Mother got back together after the war and moved out to the farm, they were to quickly produce four more children.

Doreen and Bob were soon joined by a sister Lynn and three brothers: Don, Darren and finally the youngest brother, Gill.

Father always seemed always able to find the energy to observe and supervise all of the work that he directed at me. Needless to say, his supervisory methods were comprised of negative words of profanity, a leather belt, a slap on the face or a kick. I cannot recall ever hearing even one word of praise or thanks come from him. To the contrary, whenever he spoke of any chore or other thing that I did during my childhood, his words were always to the effect that I should have done it differently and very much better and much faster.

Chapter 7

School

My sister Doreen was six years of age and I was only four when we moved to the old farm in South Mindoka. The nearest one-room school was about four miles away and across the muddy Blanche River, which was at that time, only crossed via a wooden log raft that was connected to a cable clothesline-like contraption that one used to pull the loaded raft across. As Doreen had no way of attending this school, she, and later I, did our first few years of schooling at home with our mother acting as our teacher. In Doreen's case, she went through to grade five and I completed grade three. It would not be until five years later that the District Authorities decided that the rural population of children in that particular area warranted a school bus to transport the school-age children to schools in New Liskeard, some sixteen miles away.

About three years after the our family moved onto the farm, the Townships residents also finally managed to convince the District authorities that a proper road and bridge was needed to and across the Blanche River just to the east of our farm. It was after this road and bridge was constructed that the school bus from New Liskeard began running to and from the general store and gas station that was located across the highway from where our side road began. (This store was the last stop on its highway route and was where the bus turned about). At this time, Doreen and I, along with Frank and Anne Rodgers, (who lived a few miles further back and across the river on the gravel road that went past the farm) began attending school in New Liskeard. At about this time, the old wood-frame, one-room Mindoka schoolhouse was closed down for good. In order to catch the school bus for the sixteen mile trip to the school, Doreen and I first had to get to the main highway which was about one-half mile from the farmhouse. Depending on the season and the weather, we would walk, ski or wade through the snow out the gravel roadway to Turner's General store and gas station. Turner's General store and gas station was located on the paved Trans-Canada highway, route eleven, and was as said, the last stop and the turn-around point for the school bus. This was where we children were to await the bus's arrival in the mornings and from where we walked home at night. Fortunately for we children, (especially in the cold long winter months) Turner's store always opened early enough in the morning so as to permit us to wait for the bus in the store's warm interior. As the stop was the last on the bus's long route, the driver used the store's broad driveway as a turn around, picking the children up right at the store's main door.

My introduction to a formal classroom environment was quite a significant event in my young life. I was introduced to this new environment at the grade four level at just seven years of age. Up to this point in his life our schooling and education had been done by our mother and was complemented by my considerable interest in the reading of anything I could find to read. As our mother had accelerated my and sister Doreen's home schooling, I was considerably younger than all my classmates. However, due to my rural subsistence home life, my worldly knowledge and reading skills were much more advanced than my fellow schoolmates. My first teacher, a Miss Macdonald, realizing that I might have some difficulty integrating with the other, more urban worldly children, took me under her wing, so to speak, and assisted me considerably in this integration process. I, on the other hand, had much to offer the other town-raised children who knew little about rural, subsistence farming but who always seemed eager to hear the details of my many rural exploits and adventures. I was also, because of my rough, tough upbringing, much stronger and much more ruthless than most of my fellow classmates who all seemed quite eager to challenge this strange country boy in order to establish the class pecking order. These confrontations and battles usually resulted in quite a few unwelcome trips by myself to the principal's office and a most unwelcomed familiarity with him and his wide, thick, leather hand strap. I also, while attending this old three-story brick schoolhouse became quite friendly with the school's old janitor who seemed to take a liking to me. As I displayed quite an interest in the tasks performed by the old man and in the workings of the noisy coal-fired boiler that heated the school and provided hot water for the washrooms, he permitted me access to his boiler room, showing me how the big coal-fired boilers operated. As a result of my interest, I was to spend many a lunch hour and many a recess shoveling coal into the boiler's hopper or hosing down the ice on the outdoor skating rink. The old janitor would occasionally, as thanks for my efforts and assistance, reward me with a much appreciated gift of a dollar or two as thanks.

When not busy helping the janitor or playing ball or football, I would spend all my spare time wandering around through the forests that adjoined the schoolyards. As the school was surrounded by two operating gold mines, the mines as well as the waste from the mines that covered hundreds of acres in the area provided me with much variety of terrain to explore.

* * *

Robert B. Marchand

At the ripe old age of twelve years, I completed my public school education and moved on to attend Secondary school at New Liskeards Collegiate and Vocational Institute where, two years later, I completed grade ten and began attending grade eleven. At this point, a friend (Bill Walker) and I heard that the local Ontario Northland Railway was hiring apprentice linemen and were paying the princely sum of one dollar and twenty five cents wages per hour to start. They were also, at the same time, providing room and board for only two dollars perday. This room and board was provided in hotels and included three full meals per day. For two dollars, the railways employees could eat in specified local restaurants and order whatever they wished from the restaurant's menu. This all sounded great to the boys, especially to me as it provided me with a means of escape from a very dysfunctional family life and a father that I had learned to fear and dislike immensely.

I had, previously to this time and the job with the railroad, lied about my age and worked each summer since grade eight and age twelve, on highway reconstruction work, at sawmills and as a flagman and laborer for seventy-five cents per hour wages. I was also, out of the seventy five cents per hour wages required to pay two dollars per day room and board to my father whenever I was earning a wage. I was also required to buy my own clothes, school books and any fishing, hunting or recreational items I wanted from these paltry wages. I had also, besides performing all my farm-related chores as described earlier, worked with my father doing what was called at the time, "Statute Labor." This was a means whereby any cash-poor rural Northern Ontario property owners could perform work on Township roads, bridges, culverts and other Township facilities to pay off their annual property taxes. This work usually involved brushing along the roads, ditch cleaning or the grading of the graveled roads with a horse-drawn grader. I always enjoyed riding on the grader's steel seat, operating the large steel wheels that raised and lowered the steel blade of the grader as Father drove and managed the team of horses or the tractor to pull the heavy steel contraption along the graveled roadway that meandered past our home.

Also worth mentioning, is the fact that I did, with a friend who lived in town, join the Air Cadets in New Liskeard. In order for me to attend the weekly drill sessions, I needed to stay overnight in New Liskeard which as stated earlier, was some sixteen miles away. A school friend of mine, Kirk Turner, with his parents' permission, allowed me to stay overnight at his home in New Liskeard. In return, I, with my parents' permission, invited Kirk to stay at the farm where I introduced him to the life of subsistence farm life and the sports of fishing and hunting.

* * *

Meanwhile, back to Bill Walker and my ventures into rail-roading and railroad line crews: Bill and I quit school at Christmas break when we were in grade eleven and I was about to turn fifteen years of age, to take the apprentice lineman jobs with the Ontario Northland Railway. Starting our lineman jobs in the little village of Swastika, we were soon introduced to steel climbing spurs that were attached with leather straps to our boots, heavy leather tool and climbing belts, motorized rail cars, hotel living, steam locomotives and restaurant food. I had never, in my entire life up to that point, eaten so well. The line crew, comprised of eight linemen and one foreman gradually moved north through the many small Northern communities that lay along the railway tracks, placing insulated glass and metal line-balancing brackets on the telegraph lines. As Bill and I were the most inexperienced climbers on the crew, we started our climbing on the easier to climb shorter of the telegraph poles. During one two-week period in early February while in the Matheson area the temperature constantly hovered about the minus fifty five to sixty degree below zero mark. During this extremely cold spell the line crews were unable to work on the frozen telegraph wires as they were so brittle from the cold that they would easily break if touched. The crew spent the entire two weeks huddled about barrels of gasoline permeated sand that we set on fire to keep ourselves warm. As the wires were quite taut from the cold, they could, if broken, lash out and badly injure the lineman if they struck him as he worked high on the poles.

On one occasion I began to get a little overconfident with my climbing skills and as I descended a pole one cold winter day, I drove one of my spurs into my foot. The sharp-pointed steel spur entered my foot just below the ankle, slid along the bone and exited the bottom of my foot, leaving a three inch long, three-quarters of an inch deep gash in my foot. Fortunately, it was another very cold day and as my feet were quite cold at the time, I felt absolutely nothing until a co-worker walking behind me, called out that I was leaving a trail of red blood on the snow. It required twelve stitches and two weeks compensation leave before I was able to return to work.

It was about May of that same year, that I grew tired of the constant moves from town to town and decided to quit this railroading job to take a night shift job in a sawmill that was located in the village of Swastika. While I was employed at this job I also worked and boarded on a farm in the Dane area during the day. This sawmill job turned out to be one of the hardest physical jobs that I have ever had. I was required to perform a task that was called "tailing the resaw." The job entailed taking the slabbed logs after the big bandsaw sliced a board off one side of it and flipping the log back onto the conveyor belt that returned it to the resaw for another cut. I then had to take the board or plank that had been cut from the log and flip it over to the planer man. This job did have its occasional exciting moments, especially when the big bandsaw jammed on a log and jumped off its rapidly spinning drive wheels, shooting out sparks and flames as the rapidly spinning steel saw ground to a stop from the friction of its rubbing against the hardened steel guides.

During this period I also, during the daylight hours, performed many numerous tasks on the farm where I was boarding. I would clean the stables, operate the farm tractor, disking and harrowing the big fields to prepare them for seeding. During the following year I worked at various jobs doing highway maintenance, bear and moose hunter guiding, sawmill work, lumber yard sales and as a payroll accountant for Albert Roberts at his Kenogami sawmill. The job of payroll clerk at the lumber yard was quite interesting as I had a trailer that was located on the lumber yard to live in as I sold the freshly-sawn lumber and prepared the workers' payroll. I was also required, every second week, to go out into the woods to scale the logs that had been cut by the loggers. I really enjoyed these trips as I would get to eat the deliciously-prepared foods served up at the remote logging camp kitchen.

After one and one half years of working out of school, trying to make a reasonable income and living on my own, I realized that unless I wanted to enter forestry work permanently or go into underground hard-rock mining, I should return to, and complete my high school education. It took very little convincing to get my parents to permit me to move back onto the farm as I was able to again cut the families firewood and perform the many other chores and as I was only seventeen and therefore still a minor, my parents were, by law, still required to care for me until I reached the age of eighteen.

Following this one and one half years of independence, living and working on my own I did finally compete secondary school, working each summer at various highway construction or sawmill jobs. During this period of home life I spent no more time than was necessary on the family farm. I continued to find means of escape in the surrounding forests and in assisting the nearby wildlife park owners in collecting various specimens of the local wild animals for display in the park. My knowledge of the habitant and habits of the local wildlife was also quite useful as it enabled me to become quite involved in the guiding of American bear and moose hunters. At this time in Northern Ontario, black bears were quite plentiful with a hunting season in the spring as well as in the fall. I could collect the ten dollar bounty that the Province paid for each dead bear and also get ten to twenty dollars for the bear's pelt from some passing unsuccessful bear hunter who spotted my bear hide tacked to our woodshed wall. While we never did consume the meat from the black bears, I usually managed to obtain a deer or moose for the family to consume.

* * *

My father's demeanor towards me, and to some degree, towards the other children and their mother had worsened considerably over the years. It seemed that not one day went by without some sort of dispute arising between the family and the father, with violence of some nature from the father the usual outcome. I was to finally graduate from high school two years later. I then lived and worked at a local wildlife park and as a licensed hunting guide until I joined the Canadian Armed Forces three years later.

Chapter 8

"Boots"

During the early years on the old Mindoka farm, one of the families friends, the Roberts, visited and assisted the family quite frequently. Albert Roberts had provided Mr. Marlowe with sawlogs during his earlier sawmill days to be custom sawn into lumber and the lumber then sold to his southern Ontario markets. Albert was the well-to-do brother, of the very poor Roberts family that resided in Mindoka about three miles further east, across the river, on the gravel road that ran past our farm. It was common knowledge that Albert, the successful brother, had only a public school education but had made a fortune in the logging and lumber business. His brother, however, had completed college and married a aboriginal woman only to become one of the poorest, most destitute families in Mindoka. Albert and his wife Mary would visit our family quite often to just sit, drink tea and talk. On occasion Albert would bring along a bottle of whiskey that he and Father would then consume. It was quite apparent to all, and the subject of more than a few local rumors, that Albert liked our mother very much and that she was the real reason for the many of the visits by the Roberts. There were even some unsubstantiated rumors that we older Marlowe children were at the time aware that there may have been some romantic involvement and matrimonial infidelity between Mr. Roberts and Mrs. Marlowe. There was also one rumor at the time that one of the younger of my brothers may have been fathered by Mr. Roberts.

Albert also seemed to take a liking to me. One day in early fall, just after I had commenced going to public school for the first time in New Liskeard, the Roberts were visiting our family when somehow the subject came up that I was in dire need of a pair of shoes for school wear. (I had just begun attending a real school for the first time and had nothing but rubber boots to wear).Albert, in his usual magnanimous way, suddenly said," Come on, Bobby, we are going to town to get you a new pair of shoes." Never one to turn down a offer of charity, even from a friend, Father quickly agreed to this generous offer and away Albert and I went. We were soon in the little town of Englehart, (about twelve miles north) standing in front of what was probably the only shoe store in town, looking at the shoes displayed in the shop's display window. As this was my first visit to a real shoe store, (our family normally purchased all of our shoes and clothes via postal mail order from a Simpson, Sears or Eatons catalogue) I was, understandably, quite impressed with the many styles and choices of shoes to be had. In particular, I was quite openly impressed by a pair of child's hobnailed, steel-cleated, calf-height, heavy leather logging boots. When Albert asked me if I saw anything in the window that I liked, I quickly pointed these great boots out to him and indicated that they were the only ones that I liked and the only ones that I wanted. We were soon on their way back home with me proudly wearing those heavy steel shod leather boots. What my mother said to Albert when she saw what kind of shoes we had purchased cannot readily be recalled, but whatever it was, I can be confident that it was not pleasant.

When I returned to school, I was proudly wearing those brand new heavy steel-shod boots. Needless to say, my teacher, Miss Macdonald was not, for some reason, at all impressed with my proud clomping and clacking about on the linoleum floor of her classroom. After suffering through my first day back, she thereafter made me remove my new boots before she would permit me into her classroom. It seemed to me, however, that unfortunately, the only persons who really appreciated the quality, value, usefulness and appearance of my precious new steel-shod logging boots were myself and the majority of the other envious young boys in my class. Fortunately for Miss Macdonald and all others concerned, my feet soon grew larger than those precious boots and I was forced to go back into the more conventional cheap running shoes and gumboots.

Chapter 9

"Bussing"

In order to catch the school bus once it began carrying the rural children to and from the town's schools, Doreen and I, and later, our brothers and sisters were forced to walk, wade or ski each and every school day, winter or summer, about one-half mile out the gravel road to Turner's gas station and general store, where we were most fortunate to be able, during the cold winter months, to take shelter from the bitter winter cold, inside the comfortably warm store. We then rode the school bus approximately sixteen miles each way to our school in New Liskeard. These bus rides were often quite an adventure in themselves for us children. There was always the occasional entertaining, if not bloody, fight between the Browns, the Williams and the Porter boys. At one point these fights got so out of control that the School District made me, when I was a little older, a "school bus monitor" in a attempt to quell the near riots that were occurring, ever more frequently on the bus. I enjoyed this role as Bus Monitor as it permitted me to ride in the preferred seat at the front, beside the driver and to also reign supreme over the unruly children as I now held the power to recommend suspension of riding privileges of anyone causing a disturbance.

A Father's Son

One of the more memorable school bussing times was the years of the army worm infestations. These pests were so bad one year that the school bus, on more than one occasion, was required to drive up the highway hills on the rough gravel shoulders in order to avoid the bus's tires spinning out on the carcasses of the millions of crushed worms. In addition to this slipping and sliding problem, the crushed worms, rotting in the hot spring days, created an odor that was quite unique and overwhelming in its intensity. The locals also heard from friends who worked on the Ontario Northland railway lines that the countless crushed worms on the rails made their steam engines wheels spin so badly on any sort of grade that they were required to sand the rails in order to overcome the difficulty in going up any kind of grade. Fortunately for the local residents, and the countless trees, whose leaves the worms totally consumed during their slow march through the district, this heavy infestation lasted only two years. After this time they simply disappeared with only a few minor infestations occurring during the following years. Surprisingly, the majority of the leafless trees managed to fully recover completely in the years following the "march of the army worms."

* * *

Not long after we children began riding the school bus to and from school, I discovered that many things of interest and value were to be found between and alongside the buses padded seats. As these same school buses were utilized by the bus company to carry other passengers when they not in use as a school bus many items were lost by those passengers. I was, over the years, to find wallets, watches, pocket knives, money, glasses and many other similar objects lost from the pockets of bus riders as they travelled back and forth. I soon learned that moving from seat to seat as they were vacated by offloaded children provided me with much more "loot" than by simply staying put in one seat for the entire ride home.

    During our first four or five years of riding the school bus, the gravel road that led to and past their farm home was not cleared or plowed of snow during the long cold winter months.(and after that, only occasionally when the Districts snowplows were not busy clearing the main roads). We had to, as stated earlier, walk, ski or wade through the snow out to Turner's store. Our various modes of travel, skis, bikes, or just slogging through, during the school season were completely dependent upon how deep or wet the snow was, on any particular school day. It was not at all unusual for the temperature to fall to forty degrees Fahrenheit or lower, below zero during the months of December, January and February. Doreen and I and the other children however, were seldom, if ever, kept home from school because of the excessive snow or extreme cold conditions. It was not at all unusual, and in fact it was quite common for one or more of us children to suffer frostbitten cheeks or ears during these cold winter treks to catch the school bus. During one long spell of extremely cold weather, Anne Roberts, whose family lived about three miles further back on the same Mindoka gravel road, and who also had to walk out and back every day to catch the school bus, stayed with the Marlow family for a few nights so as to avoid the long morning and evening walks in the sometimes dangerously cold weather. During these long cold winter months we children would leave home before the sun rose in order to catch the school bus for the long ride to school. Because of the extremely short northern winter days, we would not arrive back home until the long nights darkness had set in. On one very cold day following a short mild spell that had resulted in a rare midwinter thaw, the Turner stores driveway where the bus turned about had been left in an extremely icy state by the thaw. The school bus driver, driving just a little too quickly and unaware of the icy drive as he entered his route's last stop and turn around, was unable to steer the bus properly on the thick layer of ice. He crashed the big bus into the front door, the raised platform and the front wall of the Turner store, scraping the entrance door completely off the wall, crushing the platform and caving in the entire front of the store. This event, in itself, was quite exciting to all the children at the time it occurred. What made it even more exciting and at the conclusion of this event, quite bewildering, was the fact that Anne Roberts, Doreen and I were, at the time, all standing on the raised platform in front of the store's entrance door with me leaning against the outer storm door that was subsequently torn completely off the building by the force of the crash. The big heavy bus slid into the front of the store about ten feet from where we children stood waiting before bouncing and sliding into and past us, pushing in the stores front wall, completely crushing the platform and tearing the storm door completely off the wall before finally coming to a stop. The good Lord must have been watching over we three children on that cold winter day long ago as the only injury any of the children suffered was to me when the bus knocked me off the platform and rolled over my right foot as it as it bounced past us on the driveway ice.

Chapter 10

"Fishing"

It was quite early in life on our Mindoka home when I was introduced to the sport of fishing. It was probably Mathew Dawson who first perked my interest in the sport by telling me about the profusion of enormous eight to ten inch brook trout that resided in the nearby Stony Creek. Stony Creek was a small brook that crossed under the Trans-Canada highway near Mathew's home. It may also have been Richard Dumas who lived about two miles from us alongside the same small creek and who, with his wife Rose became friends of the family and who would, in the early years, visit the Marlowe family quite frequently. He also told me of the many little brook trout that resided in Stony creek and of the large delicious yellow and black walleyed pickerel that resided in the muddy Blanche River that flowed through our property about one-half mile to the east of our farmhouse. As both of these waterways were within walking or cycling distance from our home, I soon, after hearing a few good (and probably exaggerated) fishing tales from either Mathew and Richard, decided that fishing would be one of my hobbies and that I just had to catch one of those supposedly delicious fish.

A Father's Son

My first fishing trips were to the tiny Stony creek in a attempt to catch the elusive Brookies that resided in the larger of the little stream's pools. My willow fishing rod, a few feet of cheap braided fishing line, a cork bobber and a few small hooks adorned with earthworms for bait served to land me quite a few of the three and four inch lunkers before I was finally able to land a "keeper" of about nine inches in length. As I now, after catching a few of these "lunker" brook trout, considered myself a professional sports fisherman, I eventually convinced Mother and Father that an appropriate Christmas gift for a professional fisherman such as myself would be a nice new steel fishing rod, a casting reel and about fifty yards of braided line so that I would be suitably equipped for the following spring and able to provide the family with all the fish that we could eat. Fortunately for me, Mother agreed that this was a suitable Christmas gift, especially to someone who was going to keep our growing family sustained with all those fish! I was soon the proud owner of what was probably the cheapest fishing rod and reel ever made by Simpson Sears but to me, the greatest and the nicest one ever made.

A few years before this time, a steel bridge on wooden piles had finally been constructed over the Blanche River just below and to the east of our farm. This bridge replaced the dangerous old cable car contraption that had been previously used by anyone wishing to cross the river. This bridge's wide timber wing walls that served to guide the spring floodwaters under the bridge and to prevent river bank erosion now provided me with a platform from which I could stand precariously and cast out my line and fish for the large black walleyed pickerel that were purported to live there. I soon collected enough pop and beer bottles from alongside the highway to replace my reel with a slightly improved level-winding reel that I could use, after much practice, to throw a June bug spoon across the river and reel back in an attempt to lure one of these pickerel into biting. Unfortunately for me, no-one had ever told me that you were supposed to attach bait of some sort to the lures hook. After about two years of enthusiastically casting that June bug lure across the muddy Blanche, I finally did manage to catch one, and only one pickerel from the bridge using only a metal June bug spoon with no bait attached. I did discover, at a later date, that by using live minnows for bait, that one could actually catch some nice-sized fish at this location. All of the fishing adventures described thus far occurred before I had reached my tenth birthday.

At one point, when I was about seven or eight years of age, I was given a old balloon-tired bicycle by Mathew Dawson. That old bike provided me with a freedom that I had never known up to that point in my young life. I was now free to go wherever and as far as my strong young legs could pedal me. I was now, with my bike, able to go for miles up and down the main Trans-Canada highway collecting pop and beer bottles for the two cents each that they, at that time, were worth. With this newly-found source of funds I was able to purchase better fishing rods, better fishing reels, proper lines and even more and varied lures. With my bike I could now travel to bigger and better fishing spots. Crooked Creek, six miles away to the northwest for great pickerel fishing, Hough Lake, five miles away to the southwest for pike, Boston Creek to the east for trout; the world was now my limit! I was now in fisherman's heaven. Although I was still really too young to be permitted to go as far as I did on my own, I was now actually contributing to our growing family's food supplies, so my fishing trips were readily permitted by Mother and Father who seemed to have confidence in my "survival" skills.

By this time in my life, my best friend was a boy by the name of Harold Olsen with whom I was to eventually have many future fishing and hunting adventures with. In both hunting and fishing in the local lakes and forests, we were kings. We knew of all the best spots, all the best fishing holes, all the best baits to use, and the best times to go. We would ride our balloon-tired bicycles for miles up to Stony Creek or Ayde Creek to catch minnows to use for pickerel bait in the Blanche River's rapids that were below the farm home and a few miles to the north. We would also cycle many more miles to Crooked Creek or to the rapids behind the old McKenna farm. On other occasions we would bike back the gravel road behind the farm and then walk the two miles through the forest to the falls on Boston Creek to limit out on speckled trout using nothing but worms for bait.

* * *

Our old family friend, Richard Dumas also showed me many more long forgotten fishing holes in the plentiful small streams that ran through the woods of both South and North Mindoka. At the age of fifteen, I was permitted to use some of the money I earned while working on highway construction to purchase a working nineteen thirty-eight flat-head Ford car for the sum of $65.00. Not possessing a driver's license at that time, I could not persuade Father to even teach me the rudiments of driving a car. While I did have considerable experience driving a farm tractor, I had none whatsoever driving a regular vehicle. When I explained my dilemma to Harold Olsen's father, he just said, "Come on," as he led the way to his big 1955 Ford station-wagon. Telling me to get behind the wheel of this big car, Vic Olsen had me drive it down to the village of Englehart where I took my driver's test with it and surprisingly, passed after only about one half hour of prior driving experience. With this old car, Harold's and my fishing ventures now went even further afield. About this same time we discovered that "fly in fishing" was quite affordable to us. For the paltry sum of fifteen dollars each, we could have a bush plane pilot fly both of us and my little fourteen foot canvas-covered cedar canoe into some remote, pristine lake and enjoy fishing on a remote unspoiled lake with no one else around.

Over the years my ever-improving fishing talents provided our growing family with many welcomed meals when they may otherwise have gone hungry. Fishing was also, for me, another enjoyable means of escaping from Father's abuse and his ever present anger. I soon discovered that in addition to his many other dislikes, Father was extremely jealous of his young son's fishing success and would nearly always find fault with something I had done or not done. I did not fillet the fish properly, I should have caught more fish, I should have caught a bigger fish, I should not have let one get away, I should have scaled or cleaned it differently etc, etc. On many occasions I would come home from school to find my fishing gear and my hard-earned bait minnows gone. I would always know where these items could be found. I would bike down to the river bridge and find Father using my gear and my bait in a attempt to catch a fish or two. I would then have to stand and watch as, using my gear and bait, Father would catch something from the bridge and then make me retrieve the fish from the steep riverbank and carry it up to where he stood high above on the bridge. Only when he grew tired was I allowed to repossess all of my gear and whatever bait remained and then carry it, along with any fish Father might have caught, home to clean. Father never ever seemed capable of asking for the use of or of thanking me for this use of my gear, or in fact I cannot recall him ever thanking me for anything that I ever did. Oddly enough, I would have gladly permitted my father to use my gear and bait if he so wished. It was the fact that he took for granted that anything that belonged to any of us children was his if he so chose.

I learned quite early in my life that it mattered not what I did or what I might accomplish, nothing was ever up to Father's standards. During my entire growing years, I cannot recall ever hearing my father say or even indicate that he was happy with what I had done or accomplished. Nothing any of the other children in our family ever did was good enough for him or could ever meet his standards. While he was always ready to criticize what we children did or what food we brought home for him to eat, he never once in our young lives, took any of us fishing or showed us anything about fishing or hunting. Anything that I learned about fishing, hunting or trapping, I learned on my own, through trial and error, or was taught by Mathew Dawson, Richard Dumas or Harold Olsen's dad, Vic. I eventually learned to never ask Father for any information or assistance on any matter as such questions would invariably result in some sarcastic reply.

Robert B. Marchand

Chapter 11

"Forcite Fishing"

When I was about ten years of age, Father decided, for some still unknown reason, (as he only ever used it the one time) to construct a boat that was to be used on the river that ran north and south through the eastern edge of the farm's property. With my help he built what can only be accurately described as a "punt." This punt was about eleven feet in length, about four feet wide and approximately twelve inches in depth with three wooden seats. He constructed it with a flat bottom and vertical sides, all of one inch thick rough spruce boards, three inch nails and copious quantities of melted roofing tar painted on the outside but left unfinished on the inside. This cumbersome heavy wooden scow probably weighed in the area of some five hundred pounds dry weight. The "boat" was so heavy that I entertained serious doubts that it would even float but after loading it on the old farm pickup truck and hauling it down to the river and dragging it down the steep mud bank, it floated high and dry with both me and Father aboard it. We tested its seaworthiness by paddling it upstream with two homemade spruce paddles for just a few minutes before pulling it out and high on the river bank. This cumbersome "boat" was only used once after its initial launching. This use occurred on the occasion when Richard Dumas and Father decided to attempt to obtain some of the river's walleyed pickerel using for "bait" some dynamite that Father had obtained in the past for some long forgotten reason. Using Richards little two horsepower Johnson outboard motor, Richard, Father and I (I cannot recall or even imagine why I was permitted to accompany them) motored noisily up the river a distance of about two miles to a wide hole just below a shallow little rapids, that according to Richard, contained numerous quantities of the good-eating walleyed pike that frequented the river. We took no fishing gear or bait with us except for about eight sticks of dynamite, a few blasting caps, some fuse and four or five heavy rocks. We also had a stick of wax and some twine.

When we were finally floating about on the big pool, Richard and Father discussed, at length, the pools probable depth, the speed of the river's current, the river bottom's makeup and the length that the fuse should be in order to ensure the blast went off at the appropriate depth. These details were all quite critical as the length of the fuse dictated how quickly the explosion occurred after the fuse was ignited and the assembly dropped overboard into the river. It was also quite important that when dynamiting fish that the person preparing the "bait" be aware of condition of the river's bottom as its nature dictated just how much dynamite should be used. If the bottom was soft mud, the mud would absorb much of the blast so that more dynamite would have to be used. If it was rocky, the rock would reflect the blast so that less dynamite could be used.

I have no recollection of whether it was Richard or Father who had all the required technical knowledge regarding the use proper use of dynamite for our fishing purposes. However, when all of the technical details were finally worked out, the bombs assembly soon took place. Once assembled it was securely attached with twine, to one of the heavy rocks that we had brought so that the rock would, hopefully, carry the bomb to the river's bottom prior to its detonation. Father lit the fuse after ensuring that the cap was sealed against any water infiltration with a bit of wax. He then dropped the whole assembly over the side of the boat into the muddy river, whereupon Richard started his little outboard. We then motored about in a large circle around the site of the pool where the "package" had been dropped. Apparently, as Father and Richard Dumas related to me, the theory behind dynamite fishing was that the dynamite would detonate at or near the bottom of the pool where all of the fish were hopefully holding. The resulting concussion from the blast would then—again according to their theory—stun the fish, causing their air bladder to float them to the surface where we would scoop them into the boat, take them home and feast for days on all those delicious walleye fillets.

After circling about the pool for what seemed to me like an eternity, Father and Richard were just beginning to think that the water had extinguished the fuse and that they were going to have to try again. Suddenly, when they had pretty much given up all hope, a tremendous explosion slammed upwards and into the flat wooden bottom of the boat with a sharp loud "crack," seeming to lift it about six inches out of the water before dropping it back onto the now bubbling and boiling surface of the muddy river. When the river finally calmed down and the wooden punt stopped rocking about, we were finally able, (and willing) to loosen our panic stricken fingers from the boat's sides and compose themselves with Father mouthing a few of his favorite profanities and Richard simply smiling. Once we had established that we were in fact, still alive and still in one piece, and had composed ourselves, we remembered why we were there and began to look about for all of the expected fish. For about five minutes, we saw absolutely nothing on the surface of the muddy river, when, suddenly, a flash of white appeared on the waters surface a few feet from the boat.

A Father's Son

"There's one," said Richard. Then, "there's another" he said, pointing his paddle at a minnow about three inches in length that was floating belly up on the water's murky surface. Within a very few minutes, the surface of the entire pool was nearly completely covered with dead or stunned floating minnows, the majority of which soon recovered and swam away. Richard circled about for a few more minutes but nothing larger than the three or four inch minnows appeared so Father prepared a second bundle of "bait" that he tossed into another section of the big pool. After another huge explosion had further roiled the already muddy river with the same disappointing results, we motored slowly and dejectedly back down the river to the bridge without trying again. Father's only recalled comments about our forcite fishing expedition was something like – "There ain't no damn fish in that river".

A local man, Jed Roberts, who frequented the river's edge searching for anything of value that might float down from the rivers source reported a few days later that "something must have killed a bunch of minnows up from the bridge, cause I seen them all floating past." No-one ever dared tell him just what it was that caused the untimely demise of all those poor minnows.

* * *

A few years later, when I was about thirteen or fourteen years old, I happened upon the remaining dynamite hanging in a basket from the farm workshop's rafters. Ever the opportunist, and recalling all the details of my earlier experiences on the river with "forcite" fishing, I reasoned that a similar experiment was entirely possible in some remote pools on Boston Creek that often gave up, to my normal fishing tackle, some nice-sized brook trout. Looking about, I soon located a roll of fuse and a box of blasting caps. Packing up the caps, fuse, a few sticks of the dynamite along with some canning wax, I jumped on my bike and pedaled off the five or six miles down the gravel road to the trail that led through the forest to the pools on distant creek. The fishing spot I was headed for had been shown to me by Richard Dumas a few years earlier. The pools were located deep in the forest close to where the creek entered the same river that flowed past and through our farm. At this point the creek fell over a series of rock ledges into smallpools at the base of the two falls. Once I reached the pools, I decided to try the much deeper upper pool first. Preparing my "bait", (one-quarter stick of dynamite) with cap and fuse, I well waxed to make the whole assembly waterproof. I inserted the cap into the end of the piece of dynamite, tied it to a small rock and lit the fuse. I then dropped it into what I estimated was the deepest part of that particular pool. After a minute or so had gone by and I was about to turn away I heard a low "thump". A few seconds later a small quivering wave appeared on the surface of the pool. Waiting for about five minutes for the hopefully stunned trout to appear proved to be fruitless so I decided that I had not used sufficient dynamite. I decided to give the lower pool a try before giving up and heading back home. Since I had experienced no luck whatsoever on the upper pool using just one-quarter stick of dynamite, I decided that I would use the remaining three-quarters of a stick on this much shallower rock-bottomed lower pool. I soon had my second piece of "bait" prepared and its fuse lit. Standing on the rock ledge that rimmed and hung over this pool, I dropped the "bait" in the pool's approximate center and stood there, on the ledge, peering into the dark waters and waiting for the expected "thump." In about a minute or so, as I patiently and expectantly waited, peering over the edge of the ledge into the pool, I was suddenly deluged and totally engulfed by what looked, and felt like, a miniature atomic blast that consisted of the entire pool of water. Soaked through and through, I could only stand and stare in shock and amazement at the suddenly devoid of water, entirely bare, rocky bottom of the pool. In a instant, the entire pool of water, now high above me, splashed back over me as it returned to where it had originated. Needless to say, I returned home that day with soaked clothes, no fish and no explanation to anyone about how I got soaking wet on such a sunny day. I was, however, much wiser and determined to give up on "forcite fishing" forever. I never did relate the story of this day of "forcite" fishing trip to anyone other than my close friend Harold.

Chapter 12

"Stumping"

A few years after my "forcite" fishing adventure on the Boston Creek trout pools, I happened to be speaking to Chris Roberts and Mary Beersma at their cabin where they lived, about two miles from the Marlow's and just across the river from where we lived. Chris was a local subsistence farmer who had moved in with Mary and her daughter Helena after her husband Martin had left her to return to Germany. (Martin and Mary's homesteading experiences are described in a later chapter) Chris was, at the time, in the process of constructing a roadway through the forest on their property to gain vehicle access to a remote clearing that he wanted to plant in grain. He asked me to accompany him on a walk along the partially cleared bush road to show me what he was doing. While on the way he showed me a large stump that was obstructing the direct route of his road. He said that he might have to make a expensive detour around this stump as he had no easy way of removing it. Recalling that there were still a few unused sticks of dynamite left from my former unsuccessful forcite fishing ventures, I volunteered to go back home, fetch the remaining dynamite, return and blast that particular old stump out of

Chris's new road. Chris, of course, was only too happy to have me make this attempt as it would save him considerable hard work digging it out. I was soon back with the old wooden six-quart basket and its remaining contents of about seven sticks of slimy round cylinders marked "forty percent forcite." This basket had been hanging, with its contents of dynamite, in the farm's old woodshed for at least six to eight years.

Chris and Mary, their young daughter Helena and I were soon back at the stump with the dynamite. I soon had four of the sticks wrapped, fused and jammed under the exposed roots of the big stump where I thought they would do the most good, or in this case, the most damage. Figuring on quite a large blast, I inserted a goodly length of fuse, lit it and ran back with Chris, Mary and Helena to hide behind some large trees in order to protect ourselves from the anticipated huge upcoming blast.

After about three or so long minutes we heard a loud "pop" and then total silence. We waited a few more minutes and then I cautiously went up to the stump to investigate just what had occurred. Upon examining the explosives I soon realized that the blasting cap had detonated but the dynamite had not. Pondering the situation I recalled how the wooden six-quart basket that held the explosives had been badly discolored and had a odd oily feel to it. Thinking back to what I, in the past, had read about dynamite, I suddenly realized that the discolored wooden basket was probably the result of the nitroglycerine leaching out of the sticks of dynamite over the years as it hung in the shed. I then rationalized that if the wood of the old basket was soaked with nitroglycerine from the dynamite the basket itself might just be highly explosive.

It only took a few minutes before I had a blasting cap and about two feet of fuse attached to the basket that I then placed under the stump. After lighting the fuse, we all quickly raced back to again, find shelter behind the same large trees as before that were located about two hundred feet from the stump.

In around two or three minutes our world, and the big stump erupted upwards as the wooden basket, saturated with the nitroglycerine from about seven sticks of dynamite erupted in a huge blast, sending the stump and most of its root mass high into the air. Success at last! (and thankfully, the last of the dynamite)

Chapter 13

"Hunter"

At or about my ninth year of age and once Father permitted me to take out the little Canuck twenty-two caliber rifle on my own, my life changed for the better. Whatever monies I could garner collecting pop or beer bottles from the roadside I would invest in twenty-two caliber short or long rifle cartridges. The caliber depended on what I was planning to use the bullets for, or sometimes the caliber of the bullets purchased simply depended on just how much money I had to spend. If I was planning to just practice or shoot rabbits or grouse, I would use 22 shorts. If I intended to seek larger game, shoot longer distances or if I had sufficient money my bullet of choice was long rifles or extra longs. At any opportunity I would take off into the farms woods by myself or with young Danny Green, a boy who lived out on the highway about one mile from our farm and who was about my age. We would, shoot just about anything that we could draw a bead on, in or out of hunting season. Robins, sparrows, chickadees, chipmunks, squirrels, rabbits, partridges, crows, beaver, muskrat etc. Any similar bird or beast was fair game to us. As a result of all this shooting and our ongoing target practicing, I soon became a excellent shot with my little twenty-two rifle. My friend Danny would, for example, throw potatoes high in the air and

I would shoot at them, hitting at least nine out of ten of them while they were still high in the air.

I also, at about the same age, began a little trap line in the farm's extensive forests each winter where I would set wire snares on rabbit trails in order to catch them for our family's dinner table or for bait for fox or Canada lynx that I would then trap and sell to a local, licensed trapper. The local rabbits were called snowshoe hares. They changed from a drab brown in the hot summer months to a pure snow white during the cold snowy winters. During the color change phase, the rabbits were extremely vulnerable as they were often pure white against the grey/brown forest floor when all the early snows had melted due to a warm fall day. I can remember one day when Harold Olsen (another good friend) and I were hunting them, standing in only one location and being able to see at least ten of these rabbits from that one location. They were, however, very difficult to see once they were totally white and the ground was covered with winter snow.

Rabbit meat, snared and prepared in numerous ways by Mother, was a common food source for our family for many years. I would first find the rabbit trails on the snow and then I would construct a little barrier fence of twigs, leaving only a small opening that the neighborhood bunny had to pass through if he was to stay on his previously made trail. I would then prepare a small wire snare with its open noose across the opening in the twig fence with the other end of the copper snare wire secured to a tree or log. I only required five or six of these snares to keep the family supplied with fresh frozen rabbit meat. I would also, when checking my little trap line, carry my trusty rifle in the event I spotted a partridge. Hunting seasons were, for the most part, generally ignored with regards small game such as rabbits or partridge. I would not, however, hunt rabbit or partridge during the spring months when they were rearing their young. Spring and early summer was the time for fishing trout, walleyed pike or bottle collecting as described earlier.

There was also one really quite exciting day when I was about ten or eleven years old and out in the east section of the farm with my trusty little twenty-two rifle hunting something or possibly just roaming about exploring the forests. As I exited the second growth forest onto a small clearing just to the east of our house, I startled a medium-sized black bear who was busily eating fresh dandelion shoots and new clover growth at the forests edge. Thinking that I was quite the experienced big game hunter, I took aim and fired a twenty two short cartridge at this poor animal. When struck by this little lead bullet, the bear gave out a loud "whoof" and started in my direction at a fast walk. Thinking that I was a goner, and soon to be a small afternoon snack for this animal, I raced back to the forests edge and quickly made my way up to about the fifteen foot level of a small jackpine tree. Supporting myself on a branch, I reloaded another short bullet and fired again at the bruin who was now only about twenty feet away from my sanctuary in the tree. Totally ignoring the pain I was inflicting on him, the bear suddenly began to run. As I watched, now in total abject terror, the bear ran straight past the tree I was perched in. He was soon forever gone into the forest. I waited for about five minutes before climbing down and running home to relate my recent adventure to Mother, Father and my siblings. I was to eventually realize that those two twenty-two short bullets probably had no lasting effect on that surprised little bear and that he probably meant me no harm. He probably only wanted to get away from that crazy little human kid in the tree who was making so much noise and who kept stinging him!

***

When I was about twelve years of age, American black bear hunters discovered that the area that I lived in and the surrounding areas contained many large black bears. My friend Harold's step-father Sam and Harold's mother owned a nearby motel, restaurant/gas station and soon began catering to these wealthy American hunters. As Sam was a licensed hunting guide who had, up to this time, guided only moose hunters, it seemed only logical that he also guide some of these American bear hunters who availed themselves of the restaurant and motel and who also required, by Ontario law, a licensed guide. It was also only logical that Harold and I would use our knowledge of the local bear populations and their habits to earn some extra money performing guiding tasks for these hunters. We boys would take these American bear hunters out and around the countryside showing them where the bears generally located, what the bears were feeding on and then we would help them construct blinds and place out different types of baits that would hopefully entice the bears to come out of the forests near the blinds. Once the hunter had killed their bear we would then help track them down and if required, help carry them or their hides out to their car or truck.

During this same time period, the Province of Ontario had placed a ten dollar bounty on any black bears killed. Hoping to earn a little extra money and also wanting to be able to say that I had killed a bear, I finally convinced Father into allowing me to take out a thirty-thirty Savage bolt-action rifle that he had purchased for some unknown reason a few years earlier. On my second or third venture out after a bear, I decided to check out my Uncle Frank's farm field that was located deep in the forest behind our farm. As I exited the forest and looked about the big field I spotted a medium-sized black bear near the center of the field. The bear appeared to be grazing on the fresh spring grasses and tender young dandelion growth. I rested that open-sighted thirty-thirty against a small poplar tree and drew a bead on the unfortunate bear that I estimated was about one-hundred yards distance. I fired one shot. The bear immediately began racing at top speed towards me. In what seemed at the time to be about one second I had completely emptied the rifle at him with no obvious results. As he drew nearer, however, I could see bright red blood spurting high into the air from the terrible neck wound that I had inflicted on him. The poor animal finally fell to the ground dead about fifty feet from where I stood, petrified with fear as I waited for him to chew or claw me to death. I dragged that heavy bear carcass over hill and trail the three long miles home where, Father, being his normal miserable self, refused to tell me or show me anything. Our old family friend, Mathew Dawson showed and helped me to properly skin it out. I then took the skin into town where I proudly collected from the local conservation officer, my first ten dollar bounty. I then took the bear hide home, salted it down and tacked it to the woodshed wall facing the gravel roadway that went past the farm. I soon had some of the many unsuccessful American bear hunters stopping in and offering to purchase my trophy hide. I eventually sold it—and many more in future years—for twenty-five dollars each. I was twelve years old at this time.

* * *

After this big game hunting event, I convinced myself that a thirty-thirty rifle was just too small a weapon for the big game that I was after. I also did not like to have to go through the ordeal of pleading with Father for permission to use his thirty-thirty Savage rifle. Taking some of my earnings, (I was tall my age and lied about how old I was and had gotten a job as a flagman on highway construction near our home during the summer months) I placed a mail order through the Simpsons Sears mail order catalogue for a thirty-o-six J. C. Higgens bolt-action rifle with a four-power Weaver telescopic sight. My total cost was, at that time, seventy nine dollars for the rifle and thirty nine dollars for the telescopic sight. This amount of money worked out to be about two and a half weeks pay. At that time my hourly wage was only seventy five cents per hour but I was working twelve to fourteen hours per day, six days per week. I was soon the proud owner of this rifle. It served me well over the next few years, filling the family's freezer with many whitetail deer, moose steaks and roasts. It also caused the quick demise of many more black bears over those early years.

    I eventually, at the ripe old age of fourteen, obtained my own guides license and continued to work out of Sam Austen's motel, guiding and becoming friends with the many black bear hunters from the USA who returned, year after year to enjoy the area's black bear and moose hunting. In my fourteenth year, I also obtained a deer license and in early fall began scouting out suitable areas in which to hunt the whitetail deer that lived in the area. I soon found an abandoned beaver meadow on Stony Creek behind Mathew Dawson's place where I saw many fresh deer tracks and evidence of their presence. A few days after opening day I found myself crouched down behind the abandoned dam in that meadow, watching five or six deer edging out of a side ravine to dine on the rich grasses of the fertile meadow. Taking careful aim, I fired and dropped the first deer in line with my new thirty-o-six rifle. At fourteen years of age, I was now a seasoned hunter. I had successfully killed a black bear, a whitetail deer, many rabbits and many partridge!. Fastening the deer carcass to my bike presented another problem that I soon overcame with some rope and a balancing act until I finally arrived home and had the deer hanging in the woodshed. At this point I was again forced to ask Father how to proceed with the cleaning, skinning and butchering of the unfortunate deer. Father again declined to tell or show me how to proceed with this chore so I was forced to perform the evisceration on my own with no guidance whatsoever. (I did note later that Father showed no such hesitation whatsoever when it came time to dine on the tasty venison.) Fortunately, I knew pretty much how to proceed as I had considerable experience with small game animals and birds and had observed Father's earlier, butchering of our farm animals. I also knew pretty well how to proceed from my experiences cleaning and skinning black bears.

Following my success with this first deer, I was, over the next six or seven years, able to supply many meals of both deer and moose meat to our hungry farm family with my J. C. Higgins thirty -o- six rifle. In a later year of my youth I also became quite proficient with a long bow, killing one black bear and a few pesky groundhogs with it. I was eventually, over the next few years, to kill at least seven deer, eight black bear, three moose and innumerable grouse and rabbits before I left home to join the Canadian Military.

Chapter 14

"The Guide"

I was always quite big for my age so when I reached fourteen years of age, I hitchhiked down to the village of Englehart Lands and Forests office, lied about my age, and purchased, for the sum of one dollar, a Provincial guides license. I could now legally guide the American black bear hunters during the spring and fall bear hunting seasons and charge them a fee for this service. I could also guide during the fall moose hunt. This guiding service, while quite exciting, also provided me with much needed cash. For the remaining years that I spent living at the family home, I was to show and lead many hunters from the USA and Canada on both black bear and fall moose hunts. I normally hung around Sam Austen's and Ellen Olsen's motel and restaurant until some hunter would ask me to take him out and show him the best areas to hunt. For ten dollars each per day, I would go with them in their vehicle, showing them likely locations. I would also try to convince them to purchase some small pieces of cheap, smoked bacon that I would wire tightly to a tree in a good area and construct, a blind for them to wait in and watch their bait from within a reasonable shooting range. Smoked bacon, rotting fish and any other rotting meats would soon entice the hungry black bears out of the forest where the hunter could get a clear easy shot at them. On one occasion, I was asked by three African-American would-be bear hunters if I would show them the best areas to hunt as they had never been there before and had never hunted bear before. Having heard of some bear sightings on a local power transmission line, I decided to take them there.

When we arrived at the site I instructed two of these hunters to walk quietly and slowly to the north on the power line, watching for signs of feeding bears. I also instructed them on just what they should look for and what they should do if they did spot a bear. They indicated to me that they understood everything that I had told them and asked if there was any danger to them from the wild black bears. I gave them my standard answer that I always gave to all excited new bear hunters when they asked this question. I said, "All you fellows really have to know is that the northern black bear is mostly a red meat eater. And you are red meat!" This statement was usually quite successful in getting their attention and had the desired adrenalin effect on any already-frightened hunter. As these two headed slowly north, I took the other hunter across the highway and headed south on that same power line, explaining to him as we proceeded just what to watch for. This particular American hunter was hunting with a beautiful full-length stocked Mannlicker-Schoenar thirty-ought-six rifle equipped with a variable three to seven power scope. A beautiful rifle !.

We had no sooner started when we came to a small rise that overlooked a wide, shallow valley. Cresting this little hill, I spotted, about eight hundred yards away, a huge black mother bear lying on the far bank of the valley facing in the other direction. This bear's year old cub was walking about, back and forth feeding on the newly sprouted spring grasses and new dandelion greens that surrounded both of them. When I pointed the bears out to his American hunter, the man immediately crouched down as he prepared to shoot—at eight hundred yards!. I quickly whispered to him, "Not yet, we can get a lot a lot closer to them than we are, wait until I give you the okay then fire at the big one that's lying down. You should aim at her shoulder, about two thirds of the distance up on her body." I led him to about seventy yards from the location of the two bears. At this point the wet ground began to create sucking noises when we walked so I tapped him on the shoulder and whispered, "Ok, shoot from here." The American hunter knelt and aimed his rifle at the large bear that still appeared to be sleeping while her large cub continued to move about as it fed on the new grasses. After about two or three minutes he had still not fired and I could see that the cub was beginning to show signs of agitation as though he suspected something was amiss, so I said again, "Shoot."At that, the hunter finally fired but did not, after firing this one shot, move or even eject the spent cartridge from his rifle. I easily saw his one fired bullet strike the ground on the hillside about ten feet over the back of the huge mother bear. A clear clean miss! At the shot the small bear immediately sped into the forest to his right. The large mother bear however, simply stood up, gaped at us for a moment over her shoulder and then began slowly lumbering towards the forest in the same direction that her cub had gone.

"Shoot, shoot again!" I yelled at this now frozen with terror American bear hunter, "Shoot before she gets into the forest!" The terrified hunter still did not move. He stayed crouched in the shooting position with his rifle on his shoulder and his finger on the trigger of his unloaded rifle. (he had still not ejected the spent cartridge and reloaded the chamber). After another minute or so when the big bear had disappeared into the forest, he finally stood up, slung his rifle and simply said, "let's go home."

The hunter and I slowly made our way, unspeaking, back to the highway where we found his two hunting buddies standing and waiting. "We heard the shot, what happened?" one of them asked." "I don't want to talk about it," said the still frightened hunter. "Let's go home." We all then returned to the motel with my frightened hunter refusing to answer any questions put to him by his hunting pals. As we neared the motel I asked them if they wanted to go out again. They replied that they would let me know. I did not hear from these hunters ever again but later I was informed by Sam Austen that they packed up and returned to the USA the following day.

* * *

On another spring bear hunt, I took my hunter up nearby Long Lake to a recently abandoned logging camp that was apparently being frequented and broken into by hungry black bears. On this occasion, we slept in a bunkhouse that contained only one cot. The hunter slept on the cot while I bedded down on the floor beside the door.

About three a.m. I was awakened by a loud snuffing noise at the wall by my head. As I lay there, quietly waiting to see what was going to happen next, the bear grunted and ran off through the thick brush. The next morning when we opened the bunkhouse door, we found a huge, steaming pile of fresh bear dung on the platform by the door.

The following night, thinking that we were smarter than the bear, we positioned ourselves on the roof of the abandoned cookhouse in anticipation of getting a shot at the bear as he approached the camp from the forest. The cookhouse odors appeared to be the main attraction to the bears that had previously broken through the ten-test walls in many places.

At about ten p.m., just as it was getting too dark to shoot, we suddenly heard the bear walking about beneath us on the cookhouse floor. He had quietly approached and entered the cookhouse through one of the previously made holes without us hearing him. He was padding about and chewing on something good that he had found. Needless to say, when we tried to get off the roof to hopefully get a shot at him, the bear heard us and took off noisily into the nearby woods. Another exciting but unsuccessful bear hunt!

A further memory of this particular bear hunter was the fact that he possessed and drove up from the USA in a nineteen fifty six Porsche gull-wing car.

* * *

~~At~~Another time I was sitting in Sam's cafe having a coffee when two hunters came in to say that they had just shot a bear that had, according to them, "fallen" into the thick bushes at the edge of a large clearing they were watching. When I asked where the bear was now they indicated that they had not wanted to enter the brush to look for it as they were not certain that it was dead. When I pointed out to them that it would soon be dark and that it also looked as though it might rain and wash away any blood trails, they asked if I would accompany them back to retrieve their bear that evening. I agreed and we were soon on our way back to the field, accompanied by my friend, Harold Olsen.

As we approached the site, I explained to the hunters that as it was now quite dark that I would have to use a light to find and track the supposedly dead bear down. I also told them that as it was illegal to have a light and a rifle in our possession at the same time, they would have to leave their rifles in the car while we attempted to track and find the bear.

As I expected, we did not find a dead bear in the bushes at the edge of the field. It did not take long, however, for me to find blood traces on the grasses and leaves near the area where the hunters said they said they had shot at the bear. Before long, I was on my hands and knees, about one-hundred feet into the forest, in pitch blackness, slowly following the splotches of blood left by the wounded bear. I was utilizing only the light of a small hand-held flashlight with Harold and the two

American bear hunters close behind me. Suddenly, to our horror, there was a loud roaring, growling, gnashing of teeth and a crashing of bushes directly in front of us in the darkness. At this sudden noise, I reared back with a start and yelled loudly, "There he is!" to everyone and anyone who was present and wanted to listen. Unfortunately as I soon realized, there was no-one there to listen, because when I turned with my flashlight to see the reactions of my friend Harold and the two brave American hunters, all I could see was their three backs as they raced out of the forest and across the big field towards their car. (I must admit that I was not too far behind !).

We returned the following day but found only the area where the wounded bear had thrashed about and tore up the bushes, leaving nothing but blood, fur and a small piece of bone. We never did recover that particular bear.

* * *

I experienced many other similar successful and unsuccessful hunts. I was to eventually also guide long-bow hunters who aspired to shoot a black bear or a moose with their bows. This kind of hunting was generally much more exciting than hunting with a rifle as the element of danger to the hunter was much greater when a person was trying to bag a four hundred pound wild black bear with a bow rather than with a heavy caliber rifle. I spent many harrowing times on my hands and knees, following the blood spoor of a wounded bear in the pitch black of night, using nothing but a flashlight and my tracking skills. At another time I was leading Arthur, a dedicated American bow hunter who wanted to bag his bear by stalking one rather than through the usual baiting method. Arthur had made many bear hunting trips to our area and had been successful on more than one occasion with both modern day rifles and muzzle-loading, black-powder rifles. We had, on our way to the chosen hunting area, dropped off one of his bow hunter companions to watch a bait that was being consistently eaten by a bear.

After we had left him off, Arthur and I proceeded to walk north from the old South Mindoka train station to look over some large, remote abandoned farm fields in the hopes of seeing and stalking a bear as it fed on the spring grasses and dandelion greens. As evening began to fall, I indicated to Arthur that we should probably start back to where we had left our vehicle. I said to Arthur that I knew of a short cut that would take them past the other hunter that we had left in a blind watching the previously placed bait.

Arthur stated that he would prefer to go back via the same rail tracks so fortunately for us we did as he wished. Upon arriving at Arthur's car we drove down the road and observed that his friend had returned from his blind and was standing where we had originally dropped him off. We stopped and listened to him excitedly tell us that he had seen a huge black bear feeding on the meadow grasses when he neared his blind. He said that he had slipped into his blind unseen but that the bear had eventually wandered off into the forest without giving him a shot. As it was still light enough to shoot, I advised him to quickly return to his blind and that the bear, would, in all likelihood, soon return to feed on the bait. I said that we would return in about one hour to pick him up and to, hopefully, retrieve his dead bear.

After about an hour we returned to see him again standing on the gravel roadway waiting for us to return. As we pulled up beside him, I could see that he was holding a blood-covered broad-head hunting arrow in his hand and that he was very excited. He did not give me or Arthur any opportunity to ask him what had happened but just blurted out, "I got him! I got him!".

I asked him exactly what had happened and he excitedly explained, "I got to the edge of the clearing and I could see a big bear feeding on the grasses at the other end of the field so I slipped into the blind and just waited for him to get within range of my bow"."He finally got up to the bait and began chewing on it and that's when I shot an arrow at him."

"So where did you get this bloody arrow from?" I asked.

"I thought that I hit him in the chest, but he just turned and ran back down the field. I looked around where he had been standing when I shot and found my arrow lying in the grass. It must have gone clear through him." he replied. He then said that it was too dark for him to look for the bear so he decided to come back to the roadway and await our anticipated arrival.

I took the arrow from him and looked closely at it. The blood on it was quite a bright red with a few long brownish coarse hairs adhered to it. A little puzzled, I commented to both the shooter and to Arthur, "This looks like lung blood but the hair does not look like typical black bear hair." I also said that we should now go back in and see if we could find the animal as I was quite sure that it was probably dead and had likely not gone far from where the arrow had, quite obviously, from the color of the blood, pierced its lungs.

Taking a flashlight, I led the two hunters back to the blind and the baited tree. I soon found blood-streaked grasses and followed it down the field in the direction of the old trail that I had indicated earlier to Arthur was a shortcut from where we had been hunting along the railway tracks. I turned to the two hunters and said, "He was badly hurt so he probably took the easiest route away from here which is this old trail". I had, by then, lost the blood trail in the darkness so I led them about one-hundred feet down the trail where I found, lying dead on the trail, exactly what the excited bowhunter had killed with his sixty-five pound pull longbow—a fully grown cow moose !

When I showed the hunter the still-warm body of the dead moose, he vehemently denied having shot it. "I shot a bear, not a moose," he insisted.

"No," I replied, "You were so excited that you only thought you shot a bear, it would not have mattered what came up to your bait, you were so excited by then after watching it approach that you would have thought anything was a bear. If Arthur and I had taken this shortcut here earlier as I wanted to, you likely would have thought we were bears and probably would have shot at us."

My conclusions regarding this hunter were proven correct the following day when we returned and found the moose tracks in the field where it had approached the hunter's blind. It was again. the following year, proven correct when this same hunter again swore to me that he had shot at and wounded a black bear at another site. Searches of his hunting location only turned up a clean un-blooded arrow stuck in a tree behind his bait. I refused to guide this careless, excitable hunter again as I feared that one day he would kill another hunter or myself and then swear that he had shot at a bear !.

We did later salvage all the meat from this dead moose, utilizing it as feed for the caged carnivores that Harold Olsens' father had in his wildlife park.

Chapter 15

"Near Miss"

As fishing and hunting were pretty much my only recreation during my early years, I spent a lot of time doing both. They were each "a means of escape" for me from my troubled home. As it was some distance to any productive fishing areas, I more often chose to grab my rifle and head off into the nearby woods as a means of avoiding the ongoing and ever present conflicts with Father.

On occasion, or whenever the opportunity arose, I would go out with friends who had similar interests, to hunt grouse, rabbits, deer, bear, moose or just to shoot crows or whatever other small game that we came across. On one occasion I was hunting partridge with a friend in the Marquis Township area. We had stopped at the entrance to a old logging road and had exited my old Ford car. I had loaded my rifle and begun to walk down the trail when I was startled by a shotgun blast from behind. The gravel and sand was scattered and sprayed onto me as the numerous shotgun pellets hit the roadway beside my feet. As it turned out, my hunting partner, who shall remain unnamed, had accidently fired his shotgun as he was loading it. A really close one!.

On another occasion, three friends, who shall also remain unnamed, and I were breaking the law by driving around and shooting crows from the station-wagon windows with a twelve gauge shotgun. As the shotgun was passed from one side of the car to the other, it discharged inside the relatively new car, making a very large, very jagged exit hole in the car's roof. We shall never know just how our driver friend explained to his father just how he managed to blow a big hole in his new car's roof!. We think that he managed to find a friend who repaired the hole before his father found out!. Another close one!

Another near miss occurred when a boyfriend of my sister Doreen's asked me to go out with him and look over some deer hunting areas. After driving about he asked if I wanted to indulge in some target practice with his old Lee Enfield three-ought-three bolt-action rifle. We stopped at a gravel pit near the old Roberts place on the South Mindoka road and sat talking on a embankment as he began to load his rifle. As he manipulated the bolt to chamber a round, the rifle's muzzle was directly in front of my face. As he closed the bolt, the high-powered rifle, for some unknown reason, discharged, searing the right side of my face with burning gunpowder. Another really close call!

At another time, a friend and I were out target shooting with a twenty-two rifle and a old eleven millimeter Mauser rifle that had been given me by Mr. Green, a elderly Russian immigrant who lived in the woods about two miles from us. I had just fired off a round from the old rifle at a tree when my friend asked me for the now-empty cartridge. When I handed it to him, he placed it on the end of his vertically-held twenty-two rifle and fired it. When I finally arrived home that night, I had quite a difficult time explaining to Mom just how I had gotten all those slivers of lead embedded in my face! Again- a near miss! Had I not been wearing spectacles at the time I would probably have been blinded.

* * *

The only other potentially serious incident was the time I foolishly clamped a live twenty-two caliber long rifle shell in a vice clamp in our farm shop and struck it with a hammer. Just what the purpose was in doing this foolish stunt we shall never know. I did, unfortunately, following this really dumb stunt, had to then go into the house and explain to mother just what had caused the end of my thumb to disappear leaving my hand all bloody and sore! Another nearly forgotten incident occurred when I was attempting to skin my first black bear. As I was skinning out the head, I incorrectly, (as I was soon to find out the hard way) placed my knife under the skin of the bear's chin and pull it towards me. Just a moment too late, Mathew, who was assisting me said, "Never pull your knife towards yourself, always push it away from yourself as you could cut yourself badly should it slip". As he completed this sentence, the big knife slipped out from under the bear's skin and plunged deep into my shin. With my eight inch hunting knife stuck firmly in my shin bone and the dark red blood running down my leg, I hobbled into the house to receive first aid and a serious lecture regarding my stupidity from Mother.

Chapter 16

"My 80 Acres"

As I stated in a earlier chapter, Father had originally acquired two hundred and forty acres that comprised the family farm. This piece of land was made up of a one hundred and sixty acre parcel that the farm was located on and an adjoining eighty acre parcel that lay just to the west of the bigger parcel. The one hundred and sixty acre parcel was partially cleared and contained four cleared and cultivated fields of approximately five acres each. Father had clear title to this land while the adjoining eighty acre parcel, being a homestead lot, required proof of development with a minimum of ten acres cleared and cultivated before clear title could be obtained from the Provincial Government.

In order to "compensate" me for the labors performed by myself in cutting the eight to ten cords of firewood that our family used for both cooking and heating of the family home, Father verbally promised myself that once I had cleared the ten acres and he had obtained title for the eighty acres, it would be registered in my name and would then belong to me to do with as I wished. I quite foolishly believed this promise, and for many years worked industriously in the cold of winter cutting and clearing the timber and brush off this piece of land that I thought would one day be mine. Unfortunately for me, Father, bless his generous soul, did what we should probably have anticipated, and sold this eighty acre parcel of land to the farms nearest neighbor for a few thousand dollars before the ten acres was completely cleared and before he obtained clear title for it.

Chapter 17

"Poison"

An earlier chapter relates the events subsequent to and surrounding Father's unsuccessful attempts at poisoning the local wolves and foxes by saturating his dead horse with poison that he had somehow obtained. As also related, the only known victims of his poisoning efforts were the family's pet collie, Lassie and her unborn puppies. What the remainder of our family did not know at the time was that our dear father had not properly disposed of the remaining poison but had hidden it on a high ledge in the woodshed.

About five or six years after the dog poisoning episode, my younger brother Don, about four years of age and like the rest of the family children, forced to find his own means of entertainment, came into the house one day licking his fingers and to Mother's horror, holding in his hands a small opened bottle that said, on its label, in faded letters, "Poison."

This time era was when Father was still relatively healthy and was still operating, with Mathew Dawson, a small sawmill that they had located across the ravine about two hundred yards or so from where the house was located. The mill was accessed by going down the hill and then through a short trail that wound through the bush.. When Mother saw young Don licking his fingers and holding the open bottle of deadly poison, she immediately assumed the worst, grabbed the open bottle from Donny and screamed at me to, "Go get your father Bobby, Donny has gotten into the poison."

As Mother washed Donny's hands and made him spit out what he had in his mouth, I raced out of the house, down the hill and over the trail to where Father and Mathew were in the midst of sawing a large spruce log into lumber. "Daddy, Daddy," I yelled, over the sound of the big screaming circular saw, "Donny has found and eaten some of that wolf poison you hid in the shed.". I had, unfortunately, for some forgotten reason assumed that Father would care. Again, and unfortunately, he did not seem to care and totally ignoring my excited yelling, waited about four or five minutes until he had finished sawing that particular log into lumber. At that point, he went to the big Massy-Harris tractor that powered the mill, shut it down and taking three or four more long minutes, gave Mathew some long forgotten instructions about what he wanted him to do while he was away from the mill. Only then did he ask me for more about what had occurred as he walked unhurriedly to the house. It is not known, just what treatment Father and Mother then administered to poor Donny. They probably gave him something to make him vomit out anything that he might have ingested. Fortunately for Donny, the poison had either completely lost its potency over the years or he had not ingested much of it. In any event, he appeared to suffer no visible ill effects from this incident other than the severe beating he later received from Father for causing him to shut down the sawmill for about an hour.

This incident pretty well shows how interested and concerned Father was in the welfare of his children. It was only one of the many things that he either did or did not do that would eventually cause Mother and the children of our family to realize that we really did not have a father in the true sense of the word and that we could not rely on him for anything.

Chapter 18

"Pet Chipmunk"

As I will relate in a future chapter, I worked off and on for a few years for my friend Harold Olsen's stepdad, Sam Austen, who operated a wildlife park, a restaurant, gas station and motel that he had constructed at a location called the South Wye in Northern Ontario.

Early on during this time period I took on the task of catching small wild animals for the wildlife park. One of the creatures that I managed to catch was a small baby chipmunk that I took home and kept on the farmhouse porch in a old birdcage as I fed, watered and attempted to tame him.

This endeavor only lasted a very few days as I came home from work one day to find the tiny creature missing and the cage door wide open. I then asked Mother and Father if they had seen what happened to the little creature. Mother said she had not and Father said that I must have carelessly left the cage door open and that the little chipmunk pup had probably escaped.

Apparently, what had really happened, as related to me by Mother years later, was that my kind, caring father had taken the little baby animal out of the cage and for amusement, fed him to the family cat for a snack.

A Father's Son

I must have grieved terribly over this happening as I could not, later recall any part of this incident other than the catching of the little animal. What I was told about the demise of the tiny chipmunk came from Mother. The telling of this incident should serve to give the reader a somewhat better understanding of Father and of his twisted mind.

Chapter 19

"The Homesteaders"

One day, in early spring when I was about thirteen years of age, I was cycling with my rifle slung over my back about two miles back on the Mindoka gravel road that meandered past our farm. I was on my way back to check out a few fields for black bear on some of the many abandoned old farms that were in this area. As I cycled past a one of the first large old abandoned farm, I looked to the north out over the big clearing to where the old farmhouse stood. I could detect movement in the distance, so I stopped and saw someone walking across the field dragging a log. Ever curious and knowing that no-one lived anywhere nearby; I placed my bike in the ditch and walked out to intercept this unknown individual. As I neared him I could see that he was quite a small man who appeared to be about thirty-five to forty years of age. He was dragging a long weather-beaten log that he had obviously taken from the long abandoned farmhouse that stood near the edge of the big clearing. As I neared him he stopped and apprehensively, as I was carrying a rifle, waited for me to approach.

When I came up to him and said "Hi," he introduced himself as Martin Beersa and asked me if I knew who owned the property we were on.

I replied that he did not and that I thought it had long ago reverted back to the Government. I then asked him what he was doing with the log and where he was going with it.

He replied that he had moved there from Toronto after immigrating to Canada from Germany with his wife Mary and their daughter Helena. He told me that he had purchased the adjoining eighty acre property and that he now had to construct a home on that piece of property before winter set in as his wife and daughter would be soon joining them. He then asked me if it was okay to salvage the logs from the old farm house. He also informed me that he had very little money and could not afford to purchase all the materials needed to construct a house.

I replied that I had never seen anyone around there and that from the condition of the house I doubted that anyone had been there for years. Martin then took me over to where he was building his little home. It had packed dirt floors and was about fourteen feet wide by about twenty feet long. He had the log walls erected up about three feet and was currently living in a little brush lean-to that he had constructed nearby and then covered with a waterproof canvas tarpaulin.

I talked to him at length, telling him about the area, who lived nearby, where the local stores were, etc.

He did not have any sort of vehicle for transportation other than a bicycle and knew nothing at all about the surrounding area. He had absolutely nothing other than a handsaw, an axe, a hammer and nails and a few canned goods to eat. His biggest concern appeared to be that he might be eaten by a bear or a wolf before he had a chance to complete his house. He informed me that he was a gardener by trade and hoped to establish a market garden to provide him and his family with food and a living.

I was quite impressed with this little man and his plans and ideas about living in the area and starting a market garden and a greenhouse to support his family. I told him that the winters in our area were very severe and came quite early. I also told him that he had little to fear from the local bears or wolves and that I would come over and help him whenever I could. I did help him construct his little log house whenever I could and I also borrowed a soil auger from Kirk Turner that I used to drilled him a potable water well about thirty feet from his house.

By October, Martin's wife Mary and his young daughter Helena had arrived and moved into their little log house with a few pieces of cheap furniture and enough household goods to set up house. As I was well aware that they had very little money to purchase anything but the bare essentials and at times not enough to buy food, I would take my little twenty-two rifle and walk over to their house just about every weekend and try to shoot them a few rabbits or partridge for food. I also, once the first fall snows had fallen, showed Martin how he could snare his own snowshoe hares for food.

They did eventually construct a small greenhouse that they attached to their house. He had roamed about the countryside and salvaged sufficient lumber, glass and the other materials needed for this addition from the many abandoned farm houses in the area. It was difficult to understand how this little German family survived in those primitive conditions. They had no electricity, no phone, no running water, no indoor plumbing and very little food other than what I provided and what they could grow in the little greenhouse that Martin had constructed as an addition to their little house.

Martin ended up getting quite ill that first winter. His illness was apparently caused from eating the wild rabbits and spruce grouse that he had snared and that I provided them. His illness was diagnosed (or so I was told) as protein poisoning. This illness, again, so I was told, is caused by ones diet consisting of just meat that contains little or no fat, meat such as the nearly fat-free meat of wild snowshoe rabbit and partridge.

They even took for food, in the spring of the year, the meat that I would give them from any bears that I would shoot. They eventually were able to construct that small greenhouse as a addition to their cabin and produce some vegetables to supplement their diets and even had some surpluses that they sold, with me providing the required transportation and help, in the Swastika farmers' market on summer Saturdays.

I continued, as long as I was living on the family farm, to provide them with as much wild game and assistance as I could manage.

Martin was to eventually abandon his wife and daughter and return to the Toronto area and then back to Germany to live. Mary was the to "take up" with Chris Roberts, a local man, and eventually move into a small house with him that they constructed on Chris's property about a mile further down our old road. They constructed their new home on the very spot where the original Roberts home had been located. They were to live and farm there until Chris passed away some years later. At that time, Mary moved into a small apartment in Kirkland Lake to live out her remaining years.

Each and every time I returned home over the years to visit family or friends, I would always drop in to see Mary, Chris and Helena. Mary always remembered me with much fondness and would jump up and down with elation and happiness whenever she saw me. I shall always remember this tough family, the hardships they endured, their endurance and their positive attitude over the years. True Canadian Homesteaders!

Chapter 20

"Wildlife Park"

When I was about fourteen years of age Sam Austen, my pal Harold's stepfather, decided to start a wildlife park on their property at the South Wye motel. Up to this time, they had operated a motel, cafeteria and gas station. They had also accommodated and guided American and Canadian moose and black bear hunters who attempted to take advantage of the plentiful wild game that thrived in this area of Northern Ontario. The first stage in Sam's starting of this wildlife park was the construction of animal-proof fencing around the property along with numerous suitable cages and pens to house the smaller or more dangerous of the yet-to-be-obtained animals. As Harold was my best friend at the time, I spent a lot of my spare time at the Wye (as it was called) helping to pump gas, playing, fishing and hunting with Harold and cooking in the cafeteria etc.

When the park was started we spent much of our time cleaning rust off of and painting old surplus mine pipe that we then embedded in concrete and subsequently fastened many long rolls of heavy gauge six foot high fencing to in order to contain the park animals. We were also, during the same time that we were helping to construct the park, utilized in the bear and moose guiding enterprise that Sam operated. This assistant-guiding of hunters gave us the opportunity to capture or help in the capture of the young bear cubs, moose calves, lynx, deer, fox, squirrels etc that the park was to be stocked with. We also travelled with Sam to other parts of Ontario in order to purchase, from other wildlife parks or zoos other more foreign animals that were not to be found locally.

The Austen's wildlife park soon found themselves virtually swamped with the many small bear cubs that the bear hunters would bring in to them rather than kill them when they happened to shoot the mother bear. The park's first cubs, Yogi and Boo-Boo were brought to the park while during late winter when their eyes were still tightly closed and they were no bigger than small cuddly teddy bears. (and just as cute). These little animals were raised on Carnation condensed milk and regular baby food until they were old enough to consume meats and vegetables. The biggest and most challenging task of all was the successful rearing of the little calf-moose that were brought to the park or captured by Sam and us boys in the surrounding forests of Northern Ontario. Harold's uncle worked at the time for the Ontario Northland Railway as a dispatcher in the nearby village of Englehart. As a result, he would often hear, from train engineers, of moose that had been struck by one of the local trains. He would then call the park, giving the approximate location of the moose strike whereupon Sam and we boys would quickly investigate, hoping that if the moose happened to have a calf, it would stay with its mother's carcass until we could rescue it and bring it back to the park. These calf-moose were probably the most difficult of all the animals to successfully raise as no-one had any, or very little experience in the upbringing of these animals while in captivity. The park did lose two or three of these little animals before we were successful in rearing, to adulthood, Foghorn and Napoleon. Unfortunately, we were to eventually also lose Foghorn and Napoleon to a whitetail deer parasite that did not harm the host deer but was quite deadly to moose.

On one occasion, a tiny baby groundhog was brought to the park by a local resident. As this little creature was quite tiny, he was kept in a cardboard box in the restaurant's kitchen where he pretty much had the run of the entire place. This cute little creature loved ice cream. We boys would take the bottom inch or so of an ice cream cone and fill it with ice cream of any flavor and give it to him. He would take this little ice cream cone it in his little paws, stand on his hind legs and proceed, very delicately, to consume it, cone and all. Unfortunately, when he would stand up and begin to eat the tiny ice cream cone, he would gradually begin to lean over backwards until he would finally topple over onto the floor and onto his back. However, being the intelligent little groundhog that he was, he soon figured out that if his back was resting against a wall as he feasted, he could eat the entire ice cream cone without falling over. Once he had reasoned all this out he thereafter would tuck his little ice cream cone under one front leg and run, three legged, over to the nearest wall where he would stand up and lean back against it while he consumed his treat !. One smart little creature!

On another occasion, Harold and I were cleaning out one of the bear pens when one of the medium-sized semi-tame bears escaped and climbed a nearby tree. As we knew that Sam would be quite angry with us for allowing this animal to escape, we knew that we had to get it back into the cage before he found out about the escape. Unable to entice it down and back to the cage with food, we decided that I would climb up the tree carrying a rope and go up past the bear on the side of the tree opposite of where he was, until I was directly over him. I was to then drop the rope's noose over the bear's body and toss the other end down to Harold who would then drag it out of the tree and back in to its cage. Unfortunately, (or more likely, fortunately!) as I went up one side of the tree the bear went down the other side and ambled back into its pen under its own steam. Only someone who has ever handled or tried to handle, bare handed, a one hundred and fifty pound semi-wild black bear can appreciate just how fortunate Harold and I were to not get that rope on that bear!

I lived with and worked with Sam and Harold at their store and park for some years, guiding, hunting, working on the park, on the motel and the gas station. I was fortunate to be able to escape to this, my second home, whenever my real home life became unbearable. I often thought of Sam as my second father and of Harold as a brother that I could confide in whenever I needed to do so. These few years were some of the best years of my young life.

Chapter 21

"Lynx"

It was about twenty degrees below zero on the Fahrenheit thermometer on that Saturday morning long ago when I decided that the time and the weather suited going out on a moose hunt to the north, behind old Mr. Green's cabin. Mr. Green was Danny Green's Russian grandfather who had purchased some land near the area that had been homesteaded by Martin and Mary Beersa and then constructed a small one room cabin on it. Packaged myself a sandwich and a thermos of hot tea, and telling Mother roughly where I was going, I headed off on foot with my trusty thirty-ought-six rifle slung over my shoulder. It was down the gravel road about two miles to where the old trail behind Mr. Green's place led north to one of my favored hunting grounds. As I neared Mr. Green's cabin, I could see him carrying some dry firewood in through his cabin door. He spied me approaching, and as was his usual routine, invited me in for a cup of something warm. As it was quite cold on that long ago winters day, I accepted his kind offer with thanks and was soon warming my hands over Mr. Green's red-hot black iron woodstove. As Mr. Green lived by himself he was always glad for company. He then told me to help myself to a bowl of the soup that I could see that he had bubbling away, on the hot stove. I was, even though it was still quite early in the morning, soon hungrily enjoying one of my more favorite soups, barley and pork. As I emptied the bowl, Mr. Green could see that I really enjoyed his soup so he said, "Take another bowl."

I dipped the chipped enamel old soup ladle deep into the big steaming soup pot and lifted it out to pour its contents into my bowl. As I lifted the steaming ladle of soup out of the pot I could see looking up at me from the ladle, a large, staring well-boiled eyeball of the unfortunate pig's head that Mr. Green had used to form the basis of that delicious pot of pork and barley soup. With that, I quickly declined that second bowl of soup, returned the glaring eyeball back to the pot and was soon on my way north, slogging through about ten inches of newly fallen snow. Crossing two large fields, I soon located the old trappers' trail and followed it north across the beaver dam, flushing out two spruce grouse and a snowshoe hare as I ploughed along through the second-growth timber and willow brush. After traveling north through the bush for about a mile, I began to see some relatively fresh moose tracks and many Canada lynx tracks along the outer edge of a large spruce swamp. That particular year was a good one for the resident lynx population as the snowshoe hare population, the lynx's favorite food, had been on the increase for a few years. As I knew that the possibility of getting a clear shot at a moose in the thick swamp growth was probably next to impossible, I decided that sitting on a high rocky ledge that overlooked the swamp on its east side offered the best view of the area and of any moose that might be moving about, feeding on the frozen willow and poplar growth. Making my way as quietly as I could over to the rock bluff, I climbed up and was soon comfortably settled down on a cold, bare rock ledge under the sheltering branches of a lone, thickly branched spruce tree that was about thirty feet tall standing alone and well away from any other trees in the area.

After about a half hour or so of sitting quietly and seeing absolutely nothing but a Canada jay that harassed me for a few minutes, I could feel the still cold air beginning to chill my arms and upper body so I decided to eat my sandwich and to have a cup of hot tea. I soon finished eating my lunch and as I had not seen or heard anything but the occasional ravens call and the pesky Canada jay that wanted a piece of my sandwich, I decided that I would move on to a different location a little further to the north. As I stowed my remaining food and thermos of tea away, I heard, over my head in the thick spruce tree, a soft rustling noise. Looking up, I expected to see a squirrel or possibly a weasel staring down at me. I was thoroughly astonished and quite startled at what I saw. Rising quickly to my feet with my rifle at the ready I looked closely at what was actually there. Looking down at me from about ten feet over my head where they lay crouched on the trees branches with their stubby little tails twitching back and forth, were two fully grown, wild Canadian lynx. This pair of beautiful wild animals had obviously climbed the tree and hid themselves when they heard me approaching. They had now decided that they were tired of waiting for me to leave and were going to come down out of the tree even though I was still there. As these two animals skins were in prime winter condition and probably worth about two hundred dollars each to my trapper friend, I quickly rose from my perch and moved off a little to one side where I could get a clear shot at them. As I watched them through my rifle's telescopic sight, I realized that because of the way they were crouched, that I could probably kill both of them with only one shot. I leveled the crosshairs of the telescopic sight on the shoulder of the nearest lynx and slowly began to squeeze the trigger, thinking all this time of just what I could do with that two hundred dollars. As I lay in my warm bed at about ten o'clock that night, staring up at the frost-covered ceiling over my head, I wondered just what those two magnificent wild animals were doing at that particular moment.

I wondered if they could possibly ever realize just what I had given up when I took my finger off the trigger and snapped the safety back on. I slept soundly and really well that cold winter night so long ago.

I also wondered if those two magnificent wild animals were at all capable of understanding that I was really glad that I had permitted them to live for at least one more day and that I was much happier than I might have been had I continued to squeeze the trigger of my rifle.

Chapter 22

"Fly in Fish"

The following events occurred some years after I had left home and had enlisted in the Royal Canadian Air Force. My Air Force career lasted less than two years as I was forced to learn the trade of radar technician - a trade that I completely hated. I soon visited a Army recruiting center and easily passed their enrollment tests. I was then allowed to transfer to the Royal Canadian Corps of Engineers. Following my engineer and weapons training I was stationed at Camp Barriefield, Kingston, Ontario. While most of the previous related incidents occurred before I left my Mindoka home in Northern Ontario, this interesting tale cannot be left untold.

I had recently undergone serious spinal surgery after crushing two discs in a military accident. I was in a plaster body cast that encased my upper body from my shoulders to my hips and had just returned to duty after about two months sick leave. During my sick leave I had returned home to our Mindoka farm and had pretty well done as much as my body cast and my condition permitted. I had walked to and fished my favorite fishing spots and had spent a lot of my time with my old friend Harold at the wildlife park that I had helped build that was owned by Harold's mom and stepdad, Sam Austen. I was sitting at their restaurant counter one fall day just enjoying a cup of coffee when out of no-where, Sam asked me if I wanted to go on a fly-in moose hunting trip to a remote lake with him and another friend of his, Cody Walker, to fish for lake trout and hunt for moose. Being rather bored and ever ready for a adventure, I said I would love to, but that I would not be of much use as I was still in a body cast that went from my hips to my neck.

"No problem," said Sam. "You can look after camp, do the cooking and if you're able, do a little fishing and just relax".

A few days later, we loaded the canoe on the car and were soon on our way to the float plane base, some forty miles from where we lived. While on our way, we had to sidetrack to Englehart to pick up Cody from his home before proceeding to the air base. When we arrived at Cody's house we were told by his wife that he was at the grocery store doing some last minute grocery shopping for her. As we were already late, we went directly to the store to locate Cody and to, hopefully, speed him up. We spotted Cody as he left the store and told him that if we did not leave soon, our pilot would not be able to fly us into the lake until the following day as it was already getting quite late. Cody's response was to throw his two bags of groceries into our car and say, "Let's go, I will pick up my car when we get back".

As we drove to the sea plane base Sam and Cody divulged to me the real purpose of this trip. They had brought about two hundred feet of gill nets and were planning to net the big spawning lake trout from the shallows of a remote lake that was only readily accessible by seaplane or by a long six hour canoe trip.

About two hours later Sam and Cody were setting out the gill nets while I was straightening up the old trapper's cabin where we were to spend the next two nights. Later that evening, after a delicious supper of t-bone steaks that I had seared on the heavy, red-hot metal plate that lay on the wood cookstove, Sam and Cody went out in the canoe to check the recently set nets. They soon returned with about fifteen huge lake trout that were quickly gutted, wrapped and stowed away in the large trapper's pack that we had brought and placed high on a bear-proof tree platform. The following day produced another fifteen to twenty of the trophy-sized trout for the packs. The bush plane's pilot had been instructed on the trip in to pick us up at about noon of the third day so we were packed and ready to depart by eleven a.m. As we stood on the lakeshore in front of the cabin waiting, we suddenly heard the sound of a small outboard motor coming from far down the long lake. As this was a very difficult lake to access and infrequently visited, we were quite surprised that anyone else was on the lake. We waited patiently for something to appear from behind a point of land that blocked our view. I was the first to spot the canoe and its occupants as it approached the cabin. I could clearly see that it contained two men in the brown uniforms worn by Ontario fish and game enforcement officers. Sam and Cody quickly dragged the huge heavy pack of trout to a nearby pile of brush where they soon had it hidden from sight. Cody then grabbed the other smaller sack that contained the gill nets and tossing it into a hollow log, (where it probably remains to this day) began to urinate on the log as the Fisheries officers beached their canoe directly in front of where we all stood.

Recognizing Sam and Cody and believing they knew who I was, the two fisheries officers asked us how the moose hunting had been. 'Not too good," we replied, "but we did hear some shooting yesterday coming from further down the lake." The fisheries officers spoke to the three of us for a few minutes, looking about the camp area as they spoke. "Do you mind if we use the cabin to warm ourselves and to heat our lunch?" they asked. "Of course not," Sam replied as the seaplane landed in front of them and began to taxi over to our location.

At that point, and really having no choice in the matter, we secured the canoe to the aircraft's pontoons, loaded our gear on board, (with the exception of the hidden pack of fish that was still out of sight under the brush pile) boarded and were soon in the air and on our way. As we flew out we discussed just how we would go about getting our big sack of ill-gained fish back and if they, the two enforcement officers really knew what we had been up to. As it was quite a long canoe trip out from the lake for the fisheries officers, we decided to hide in the forest at the location that we knew the officers would eventually have to come to in order to get to their vehicle. We decided that if they did not have the fish with them, that we would fly back in to the cabin and retrieve them and the nets. After what seemed like forever, the canoe finally appeared, the fisheries officers disembarked and straining, lifted the heavy pack full of our fish out of the canoe and into their truck. Looking at each other, we decided at that point that we would follow the fisheries vehicle out and if they stopped for any reason, that we, the poachers, would attempt to steal our fish back from their truck so that they would have no evidence of our lawbreaking enterprise. Unfortunately, or possibly fortunately for us, the fisheries officers did not stop and give us the opportunity to further break the law so we went home, figuring that if we did not see the fisheries people in the next few days that we were safe from prosecution.

Approximately two or three days later, I was sitting at the cafe counter in Sam's restaurant drinking coffee when in walked a number of Provincial fisheries officers who declared that they had search warrants authorizing them to search the premises. I soon realized what was up and hurried home to see if they were also searching my parent's farm. They were not. I returned to Sam's restaurant later that same day to discuss the day's events with Sam. Sam informed me that the Fisheries officers completed their search but had found nothing of interest at his place. He also related that Cody Walker had phoned to say that fisheries officers had not just searched his home but they had also searched his brother Mel's home where they had found a large lake trout with net marks on it in his freezer. It soon became clear that the Fisheries people had mistaken me for Mel's son, who was about my age. Thus the reason for searching his home rather than mine. It was also rather humorous that the only fish that the officers ever found was in Mel's possession. Unfortunately Mel's wife had just recently, but legally, purchased the discovered lake trout from a travelling commercial fisherman from Quebec who frequently traveled about Northern Ontario selling his legally-caught lake trout.

As it appeared that I was in the clear and my sick leave was over, I reported back to work at the military base in Kingston about three weeks later. I was busily working away at my drafting desk one day (I was now in a full-body back brace that had replaced my body cast) when in walked a fisheries officer to serve me with a court summons to appear in front of the local magistrate in my home area of Kirkland Lake, some four hundred miles away, the following day at ten a.m.

I quickly spoke to my Sergeant Major and arranged for time off. I then immediately drove back to Kirkland Lake to find that Sam, Cody and the innocent Mel had also been served with summons to appear in Civil Court in Kirkland Lake on the same date and time as I. The three poachers had already retained a local attorney for a hundred and twenty dollar fee each, who proceeded to assure us all, that the Fisheries Department had only circumstantial evidence and that unless the bush plane pilot testified against us, that all four of us would be quickly found innocent. When we arrived in the courtroom we found it jammed with spectators. It apparently was well known by the town's citizens that some prominent locals were to be tried that day for illegally netting fish. We also saw all of the lake trout, frozen solid, lying on the floor of the courtroom beside the Magistrate's bench.

As the Magistrate sat down, he commented on the "three hundred and eighty pounds of frozen fish that would soon thaw out unless this particular case was soon dealt with." With that comment, the courtroom spectators all roared with laughter and the three of us guilty ones began to realize that we were only there to observe our conviction. The Magistrate asked us individually how we were pleading. Sam, Cody, Mel and I each, in turn, stood and said, "not guilty," as the crowd again roared with laughter. (We now fully realized that we were all sunk) The Magistrate questioned the fisheries officers, the pilot (who said nothing that would incriminate us) and a fisheries biologist at length before finding all of us, with the exception of Mel Walker, "Guilty as charged, I sentence you to a fine of one-hundred dollars and costs of ten dollars each". Followed by the loud raucous laughter of the crowded courtroom, we dejectedly left the court, paid our fines and went home.

Chapter 23

"Blue"

This next story is quite unpleasant and difficult for me to relate. The reader may choose to not read further as the happenings might cause even the strongest of souls to hesitate. I have found it extremely difficult to forget this incident or to forgive myself for what occurred on that long ago day. I am equally sure that the good Lord may not forgive me as well.

***

This story begins one fall morning during early deer hunting season when I was about fourteen years of age. Usually the first to arise, I went down to let the family's pet dog out for her morning toiletries, to start the cook-stove fire and to prepare Father's tea. As I did so, a large strange "blue-tick" hound greeted me at the door with a wagging tail and some friendly licks to my face. A beautiful, friendly animal, I immediately took a liking to him. He also seemed quite comfortable with me and the rest of the family as well. As our family already had a dog and a couple of house cats, Mother and Father felt that they could not keep and feed this animal so they posted "found dog" signs in all the nearby public places. When, after a few weeks they still had no response to these notices, they took advantage of a free offer and posted a found dog notice in the Northern Daily News, a paper published in Kirkland Lake. After another week or two had gone by and they still had not received any word of a missing dog, it became decision time. Our family first tried to give the animal to anyone who would take him. No luck. They then thought they would keep him but he kept scratching huge holes in all of the house screen doors and even in the porch window screens. It was apparent that his owner had permitted him access to the inside of their house as he made every possible effort at every chance to get in our home. It finally came to the point where Mother said to me, "You will have to take Blue (as we had named him) out and shoot him before he wrecks the house completely."

There was no way that I was going to kill that pretty blue-tick hound. Blue had really grown on me with his easy-going, friendly manner and I kept hoping that someone would come along and claim him as theirs. Time passed into late fall and Father as well as Mother kept telling me that the family could not afford to continue feeding this stray animal that was always wrecking the farmhouse window screens and doors with his persistent scratching as he attempted to gain entry to the warmth of the house. I could not bear the thought of having to shoot this animal as I had previously had to do with many of the family's pet dogs that had been injured by passing vehicles or had become chicken killers. The idea of calling animal control or the local dog pound was out of the question in our area as both were non-existent in those long ago days. This sad chapter in my youth came to an abrupt end one afternoon as I was trudging down the Mindoka side road headed out for a late fall moose hunt. As I walked along the gravel road, I suddenly saw Blue racing through the woods to my immediate right, about seventy-five feet from the road in the bushes. I knew that as long as he was not tied up he would continue to follow me and that my moose hunt would be fruitless. I thought about how I could get the animal to return home but I knew that as long as the dog was loose, that he would remain with me and, spoil my hunt. I then began to think of Mother's and Father's previous directions about getting rid of him and thought, "This is my opportunity, I have my gun, we are away from the house, he is now a problem to me and I can shoot him in the bush where he is without having to get near him and look at his soulful eyes."

Without further thought, I raised my thirty-ought-six rifle to my shoulder, lined up the cross-hairs of the scope on the running dog and fired. Blue let out a yelp, tumbled over and then was quickly up and running back towards the farm house. As I had expected the heavy caliber bullet to kill him instantly and not just injure him, I hurriedly ran home with a sick feeling to where I knew that Blue would go if he was injured and at all capable. I arrived back to find him lying on the porch looking up at me accusingly with his sad soulful eyes. A patch of skin about six inches square was completely missing from the top of his shoulders where the heavy caliber bullet that had just grazed him, exposing all of his shoulder muscles and tendons. Not wishing to allow him to suffer further I quickly returned my hi-powered moose rifle to its rack and grabbed my twenty-two caliber rifle and a few cartridges. I then tied a short length of rope to poor Blue's collar and led the still trusting animal slowly across the east field to the edge of the forest where I tied him securely to a small tree. Stepping back a few feet, I said to him, "I'm really sorry, Blue," and fired three bullets into the dogs head. Blue went down immediately and did not move.

I returned to the house, put up my rifle, grabbed a shovel and headed back to give Blue a decent and proper burial. As I neared where he lay, I could not quite believe what I was seeing. Blue was sitting up, still secured to the tree, with blood streaming down and over his face and calmly looking up at me as I approached as if to say, "Why did you do this to me?" Obviously, the twenty-two bullets had not fully penetrated his skull and brain, but had just bounced off and rendered him unconscious for a few moments. At that point I threw down the shovel and raced back to the house with tears streaming down my face to again grab my rifle and more shells to return and finish the mess I had created.

Mother saw me as I left the house and yelled after me, "Bobby, what's the matter, why are you crying ?" I did not reply but quickly returned to Blue where, still sobbing, I asked him for his forgiveness and then finally, killed him.

I did not sleep very well that night or for many more nights, as I said to myself many, many times over, "Please forgive me Blue, please forgive me". After all these years I still think often about that pretty blue-tick hound and still, on many the occasion, ask him to forgive me.

Robert B. Marchand

Chapter 24

"Hasenpfeffer"

As related in a earlier chapter, one of the farm chores that I voluntarily undertook during my youth was to provide the family with as much edible wild meat and fish as I was able. One of my methods was to establish, each winter, as soon as the first snow appeared and stayed, a little trap line of snowshoe rabbit snares. As the snowshoe rabbit population fluctuated from year to year, the numbers of rabbits I caught would also fluctuate. Mother usually prepared the rabbit meat much as one would prepare ordinary chicken. Fried, roasted and stewed rabbit meat was common household fare, especially after the family had consumed all of their domestic chickens, ducks and geese. One winter, after eating endless meals of wild rabbit meat, Doreen and I harassed Mother long and hard to get her to prepare a different dish than was normal from the wild rabbit meat. Her answer to our pleas was to find, in one of her cookbooks, a recipe for rabbit called "hasenpfeffer." This recipe involved taking the pieces of rabbit meat and marinating them in some quite strong smelling marinade for three or four days. What we all soon discovered to our dismay, was that the odors that this concoction emitted became more pungent and stronger with each passing hour as it basted in the marinade. Fortunately for Doreen and I, we were attending school in Kirkland Lake at the time and were away from these terrible odors for much of the day. Not so for Mother, Father and the younger children. By the time the meat was sufficiently marinated and ready to cook, they were all clamoring for Mother to throw it out. Unwilling to waste her efforts, she refused and ended up cooking the meat as directed by her recipe. As Doreen and I were at home when she finally cooked this meal of marinated rabbit, we also had to undergo the torture of smelling the even more terrible smells of the marinated meat as it simmered in the woodstoves oven. Doreen and I would later both agree that this meal of "hasenpfeffer" was and still is the best-tasting meal of rabbit that we have ever had! Unfortunately for us, Mother never again made us this delectable meal of marinated wild snowshoe hare !.

Robert B. Marchand

Chapter 25

"Arsonist"

One of my many means of amusement and of getting the most use out of what was on hand, was my saving all of the empty twenty-two cartridge cases from my many shooting adventures. These empty bullet cases could be filled with the rounded flammable striking ends of the large wooden matches of those days. A adventuresome person such as myself could now take these, "recharged" twenty-two cartridges, place them on a rock or other such hard surface and strike them mightily with another rock or hammer. The size of the ensuing explosion was usually directly in proportion to the number of match heads that one had managed to stuff into the empty casing. On one occasion, on a hot dry summer day, when I was about eleven or twelve years of age, I was on my way out to Turner's store and gas station to get Mother or Father some tobacco when I stopped on the rocky hill that was situated about midpoint between the farm house and the store. I had, in my pocket, six or seven of my little "explosive devices" and decided to blow up a few of them on the rocky hill. After satisfactorily detonating them, I was soon continuing on my way to the store.

A few minutes after arriving at the store, Old Mr. Morgan, a retired gentleman who was a good friend of the family and who lived with his elderly wife, just across the highway from the

A Father's Son

store, rushed in to inform us that the forested hill on the gravel road that led to our home was on fire. Within about an hour, forestry firefighters were on the scene courageously battling the now fully involved fire. The firefighters, thank goodness, did finally extinguish the fire before it had burnt more than about four or five acres of the scrub forest that covered the hill. When the fire was finally out, the forestry people questioned all those present at the store at length in a attempt to find out what had caused the fire to start. When they questioned me, I told them, in as innocent a manner as I could muster, that when I had passed over the hill about one hour before the fire was noticed, I had seen nothing unusual. They then questioned Mr. Turner, the store's owner, who knew nothing about what had occurred, and said as much. When they then questioned Mr. Morgan however, he said to them that he had been working in his yard and had seen everything. With this statement, I thought, "My goose is surely cooked, I'm going to jail!" I knew that the source of the fire had to be one of my little exploded homemade "bombs" and that I was completely and in every way responsible for the ensuing fire.

Old Mr. Morgan's next statement and actions clearly described his friendship and his sense of humor. Winking broadly at me he said to the officials, "After I saw young Bobby come over the hill, I saw some guy who I had never seen before come out the road behind him."This guy stopped on top of the hill, and I saw him sitting down on that big rock up there, probably to have a smoke. That's probably what started the fire, that guy's cigarette."

I was soon on my way home, extremely relieved and extremely thankful that I had a friend like Mr. Morgan.

Chapter 26

Brothers and Sisters

As stated earlier in this story, I had one older sister, Doreen, who I nicknamed and fondly remember calling (to her chagrin) "Diddy". As related in a earlier chapter, Doreen and myself were pretty much used as child labor by our father while we, the children, lived on the farm. Beatings, threats, putdowns and other physical abuses were to us, normal. I was, in many ways, much more fortunate than Doreen in that I could, once I was old enough and able, to escape those abuses by going out into the South Mindoka wilderness with my trusty little Canuck single-shot rifle whenever the situation at home became intolerable, whereas she could not.

I began working on highway construction projects in our area by lying about my age when I was about twelve or thirteen years old and Doreen began working in the South Wye restaurant at about the same age. Following Father's return from the War and the move to the farm in South Mindoka, Father and Mother were to have four more children.

* * *

Lynn was the first to appear. She was as normal as could be but I cannot recall if she was born in the farmhouse or in a hospital. I do remember that when one of the children was about to be born in midwinter one year, we had a terrific snowstorm and when Father tried to get the horses and a sleigh from the barn to the house so as to get Mother out to the highway where she could be taken by car to the hospital, the horses went down in the snow and could not, or would not rise. Father could not get them to stand no matter what he did so he was forced to cover them with heavy blankets and hand carry hay, water and feed for them in order to keep them alive during the extreme cold. I can also recall that he built a huge bonfire on the snow nearby in an effort to keep them from freezing. In any event this was probably the time of my sister Lynn's birth at home on the farm. After about a week or so Father managed to get the team of horses up by constructing a pole tripod over them and using a block and tackle, hoisted them up and onto their feet.

Lynn's biggest claim to fame while growing up on the farm was the time she slammed a interior house door on a young kitten, causing it to scream out in pain. I, being the nasty mean older brother, made quite sure that she believed that she had killed that kitten by tormenting her with that suggestion until she actually believed it. As there were a few other kittens running around the house and Lynn was still quite young, this deception was easily done. I did not realize until many years later, that my deception about her killing the kitten was so complete that she, even years later as an adult, still thought that she had. (You did NOT kill that little kitten, Lynn!) Lynn, for whatever reason, seemed to be favored by Father much more than the rest of the children were and received much less abuse from him over the years. Lynn also worked, as did sister Doreen, at the South Wye Restaurant during her teen years. I believe that I was also the only member of the family that was required to pay my parents for my room and board whenever I was working for a wage at a outside job. Lynn, like Doreen, was to move away from the family home as soon as she was able.

Don was the fourth child and the second son born to the family. Don was also born at the farm and was quite fortunate to survive his birth as he was born a "blue baby", whatever that means. Don was, next to me, the child who was also picked on and tormented by Father. Don was always a "follower" and was easily led and influenced by others during his formative years. My fondest memory of Don occurred on one Christmas Eve when he was about nine or ten years of age. Mother was reading a Christmas story to the younger children by the light of a dim coal-oil lamp, and I had just scolded my younger siblings about Santa's not coming with their presents until they were all abed. A few minutes after the scolding, I sneaked quietly out the back door into the cold winter night. Making my way around to the front door that opened into the room where everyone was seated, I placed my face near the door, and in the dark of that Christmas Eve so long ago, said loudly, "Ho, ho, ho, Merry Christmas!."

According to Mother's later comments, Don's reaction was instantaneous. He leapt to his feet and yelled, "There's Santa!" He then raced up the stairs to his bed, leaving Mother and the remaining children sitting in the living room. Another recollection I have of young brother Don is about the day that Mother decided to have a small picnic up on the rocky hill beside the farm house. Don was only about a year or so old, and for whatever reason, was nude from the waist down on that warm summer day. As was normal at the first sign of food on the farm, the many local yellow-jackets soon began harassing the group of picnickers as we munched on our sandwiches and drank our cool-aid. The family was soon made aware by young Don that the wasps did not really appreciate his nudity when one of them stung him on his little penis, ending the family's picnic on the rocks. I always enjoyed, after we children had left home and gone our separate ways, seeing and speaking to Don in later years. Don always seemed to me to be a "lost soul," a lost little boy searching for approval from others or for an elusive something in life that I sincerely hope that he eventually found. He was, later, to perish in a automobile accident while on his way to work one cold winter morning. "I miss you, Don." I always miss Don and miss hearing of his life's adventures, of which he, like the rest of the family, had many.

The fifth child born into the family was my brother Darren. For some reason and as best as I can recall, Father seemed to leave Darren pretty much alone. Perhaps that was because he had used all his abuse up on the older children. Darren was to be the intellectual child of the family and was to be the only member of the family to, on his own, finance, attend and graduate University with honors. As Darren was much younger than me, my recollections of his younger years are spotty at best. I do recall a episode when Darren was about three or four years of age and playing shirtless in the farm yard. The first indications that something was wrong was when the family heard Darren's screams and the loud honking of our flock of geese coming from the back yard. Rushing out we could see young Darren on the ground, surrounded by the entire flock of our tame geese. They were honking madly and pecking away at his bare tender back and shoulders. I can also recall that Darren was, to some degree, allergic to the countless black flies, mosquitoes and sand fleas that populated the farm each and every summer. During the summer months his chest would be a mass of scars from his relentless scratching of the countless itchy bites on his young body. Darren went on to become not only successful in his adult life as a teacher but also to be well-liked and admired by all those who know him. In this next paragraph, I will attempt to describe Darren's character to the reader.

I was to ask Darren if he would like to come with me one fine sunny spring day when I was hunting for black bear in South Mindoka. As it turned out, I was the only member of the family who became enamored with the sports of hunting and fishing. On this particular day as we neared a power transmission line and knowing that these locations were excellent places to spot spring bear as they fed on the tender early grasses, I parked my old nineteen thirty-eight Ford coupe on the side of the old narrow gravel road. We then headed off down the open right of way with me leading the way. As I cleared the first rocky ridge I spotted a large mother bear in the open about fifty yards ahead with her two young cubs loudly frolicking nearby in the forest. Crouching down, I signaled back to Darren to come up and take a look as I prepared my rifle to shoot. When Darren came forward and observed the mother bear and her cubs, he simply looked and said absolutely nothing. As I knew this was the first time that Darren had ever seen a wild bear in its natural environment, I expected that Darren would be quite excited. To the contrary, he said nothing at all so I assumed that he could not see the animal from his location.

"Don't you see them?" I asked.

"Yes," Darren replied, quite calmly. "I see her."

I was so taken aback by Darren's display of calmness that I could not shoot that mother bear in front of my young brother on that long ago day. I was very proud, that day, of my brother.

The sixth and last child born into the Marlowe family was Gill. Again, I cannot recall that Gill was picked on or abused to the same extent as were Doreen, me and Don. He may have been subjected to some, but like Darren, he was so much younger than I that I cannot confirm that he was or was not. Again, due to the fact that I attempted to escape as often as I was able from the family home and was quite a bit older, I cannot recall much of Gill's early childhood.

I can recall one occasion when I took my brothers Don, Darren and Gill back to one of my favorite trout fishing holes on Boston Creek. This spot was quite a long bicycle trip from the farm home and since I intended to spend the night camping on the creek, the group of us boys were quite loaded down with blankets, fishing equipment and other gear. As the weather seemed fine when we left home, we took only the barest of gear. We had no tent or tarp to protect us from any possible rainfall or foul weather. I also wanted to make the trip a real adventure for the boys that they would have no problem remembering.

Upon arriving at the falls, we laid our bedrolls out under a tall thick spruce tree that would offer some overhead cover in the event it rained. We enjoyed some pleasant fishing time although we had no luck whatsoever. Catching fish, however, was unimportant to the boys as they seemed to be having a great time. As the sky began to darken with the onset of nightfall, I told the boys to get into their bedrolls as I did the same. They did so and before long we were all fast asleep.

At some point in the night it began to rain. I was awakened by the drip, drip of water on my bedroll, so I quietly rose and moved myself to the opposite side of where the boys were as it seemed a much dryer location. After a not too pleasant a night, we all woke at about the same time to a dreary dull, overcast morning. To this day I can still recall Gill's apparent amazement at just how his older brother could have mysteriously relocated his bed's position during the night. What was just as amazing to myself was the fact that Gil waited until days later to express to me and to our parents, his utter bewilderment at just how his brother Bob seemed to magically move during that rainy night.

After reviewing of all of my brothers' and sisters' and my own life to date, I now realize that we all had much in common and had many of the same difficulties with everyday, common life skills. All of the family children seemed to have all had problems with relationships. We all, had trouble expressing and or displaying our innermost feelings and emotions towards others. I have often said to friends over the years that I always have believed in the old adage, "We are what we eat". In a like manner, I believe that, "We are what we have seen and experienced in family during our formative years. We are what we have been taught by our parents," or "We are what we were shown by our parents as we grew and developed during our formative years." I also told my brothers and sisters many years after leaving home that I could not remember ever being told by our parents that they, our parents, loved us or cared for us in any way. We children and our mother were, in my opinion, simply tools or servants to be used and manipulated by our father. I cannot remember anything at all that was enjoyable in my life during my years on that South Mindoka farm with the exceptions being the times that I was able to escape out into the forest or the times our father was away. I believe, or would prefer to believe that our mother was unable or incapable of bringing to bear any influence on our father regarding our upbringing. I do know that, and personally witnessed many abuses, physical as well as mental that Father heaped upon her.

Chapter 27

"A Clear and Easy Shot"

As stated in a earlier chapter, as soon as I was able to find the money, I purchased a Simpsons Sears J.C. Higgens thirty-ought-six bolt-action rifle for my use in my hunting of bear, dear and moose. Until then I was forced to pretty much beg our father to let me use his Savage bolt-action thirty-thirty for any big game hunting. I was to become very proficient and an accurate shot with this high-powered and deadly weapon. I could easily keep all of my fired rounds inside a one inch group at one hundred yards distance. On one occasion I aimed at a crow's head at about two hundred and fifty yards with the bullet striking the unfortunate bird exactly where I had aimed. On another occasion I shot and killed a Canadian lynx from the farm house's back porch at about three hundred yards distance.

One fine fall day as I was returning from a hunt on our farm property, I came to a nice-looking resting spot on the edge of the second clearing north of our farmhouse. This site had a good overview of the remaining fields and also provided a clear view of the house and its yard. The house was just across the ravine that separated it from our old log barn and was about two hundred and seventy-five yards from where I was sitting. As I had, on occasion, seen whitetail deer in these fields, I decided to "hunker down" for a while and watch for game movement and possibly get myself some deer meat that was within easy carrying distance of our house. I was in no hurry to return home that day as I had, earlier in the same day, suffered abuse of some nature at the hands of Father for some long forgotten reason and I did not look forward to getting home and renewing this conflict. As I sat, quietly reflecting on the day's events and looking about for any signs of movement, I noticed someone in the distance, moving about the house yard. Perceiving that this person in the yard was Father, my rifle quickly and with no conscious thought, came to my shoulder where my eye soon placed the crosshairs of the rifle's telescopic sight on the bottom of Father's neck. At that range, the two hundred and twenty grain soft-point bullet would hit him dead center in his chest and would probably turn both his heart and lungs instantly into a bloody mush, killing him instantly. As I followed Father's movements around the yard with the high-powered rifle's crosshairs, a million thoughts raced through my mind. How much better off we would all be, no more abuse, no more beatings, no more servitude, no more mental anguish, no more of having to protect Mother from the physical and mental abuses that he heaped upon her. As all these thoughts raced through my mind, my thumb snapped off the powerful rifle's safety and my finger began to slowly tighten around the trigger.

I can still, some fifty-five or so years later, quite clearly remember the events of that long ago day. What I cannot recall, is just what it was that stayed my shot. I firmly believe that whatever it was that held me from putting the final bit of pressure on my rifle's trigger and prevented the death of Father could only have come from our Lord.

A Father's Son

Chapter 28

"Abandoned Homes"

As stated in an earlier chapter, I began quite early in my life to roam, first on foot and then by bicycle, as far from home as whatever my mode of transportation at the time would permit. When I obtained and became reasonably proficient on a bike, the distance I could travel became suddenly much more considerable, opening a considerably larger territory for me to explore. I would often rise early in the morning, take care of whatever chores I had to perform, pack a little food, grab my little twenty-two Canuck rifle or my thirty-ought-six and head off. I would usually ride off to the east of the farm, down the gravel road and across the muddy Blanche River. This direction was the best for exploring as the remote area was full of overgrown abandoned fields, abandoned farmhouses, barns and other outbuildings. Many of these abandoned homesteads were situated in what at first glance appeared to be in the middle of the forest. Some on-foot exploration, however, would usually reveal a old overgrown path or dirt horse roadway originating on a currently-used road or to one of the two abandoned Ontario Northland Railway "Whistle Stop" stations. Signs were still visible at this time long ago identifying these old stations as "North Mindoka" and "South Mindoka."

Questioning of some of the remaining long-time area residents revealed considerable information about these old train stations as well as some of the history of the long abandoned farms. It seems that in the early years of the Great Depression of the nineteen-thirties, many Canadian and immigrant families were forced by the unemployment to move to the rural areas of Northern Ontario and begin farming simply in order to exist and have enough food to eat. These hardworking families would take out homesteads, move onto the land, construct a home and accessory buildings, clear some land and somehow obtain a horse and other farm animals. By growing their own vegetables and meats and by harvesting whatever foods the wilderness had to offer, they were able to survive and thrive during those terrible years. (All this sounded a lot like our own life on the farm) As this particular area was isolated at the time by a un-bridged river and long distances, the Ontario Northland Railway, passing through this remote area, became these enterprising homesteaders savior as the Railroad Company, when the need arose, established the two "whistle-stop" stations at North and South Mindoka. The existence of these railroad stations explained why the majority of the once-occupied homesteads were within reasonable walking distance of them. With no other means or methods of travel, being within a reasonable distance of the railway was essential to those twentieth century pioneers.

The reason, as was related to me, that all of these remote subsistence farms were eventually abandoned was also quite simply explained. As Canada's involvement in World War Two increased, the majority of the young men who were working these subsistence farms, left and went off to enlist in the Canadian or the English Military forces. As a result of this exodus of the majority of the young working men, the families left on these remote farms soon found themselves unable to manage without the help of the young men who had gone off to enlist. It seems that, within two years of the war's onset, or about nineteen-forty-one or forty-two, the majority of these farms had been abandoned and with the remaining occupants having moved into the surrounding villages and towns. In many cases, the farms occupants simply walked away, leaving their furnishings, household goods and even much of their personal items behind. When one realizes the remoteness, the lack of transportation, the long cold winters, the lack of money and the terrible loneliness that the left-behind families had to endure, it becomes obvious that they had no choice at the time but to move out. I am sure that many of these families, when they left the homesteads, intended to return to their homes when the war ended. They had, as I was also sure, no idea at the time that the war would last for some of them some seven years and for many others, forever.

In any event, and back to my story, many of these old abandoned homesteads when I first found them in the early to mid nineteen-fifties were, except for about twelve to eighteen years of unoccupied ageing, almost exactly as the owners had left them those many years ago. In at least one of the old farmhouses, even the dishes were still located on the old homemade kitchen table where they had been left by the sudden departing of the family. If only the crumbling walls of those old farmhouses could have spoken!. As I examined these homesteads, I felt sure that each one of these old homes and farms were some persons or some family's hopes and dreams at one time.

Even though these old farms were quite obviously long abandoned, I still felt quite uneasy going through them and examining old papers, books, furnishings and the like. Looking back at these long ago times I now realize that I could have taken and sold as antiques much of what had been left behind by these long gone souls. In reality, I took very little as I would always be thinking, "What if these people decide to come back?" Of course they never ever did return, and when I returned to these old remote abandoned homes many years later they had all been looted or ransacked and in the majority of cases, disappeared altogether.

Robert B. Marchand

Chapter 29

"43 Mauser"

As mentioned in a earlier chapter, an old Russian or Polish immigrant to Canada, Mr. Green (I am quite sure that "Green" was not his Russian surname) lived nearby the Marlowe farm further back on the South Mindoka road just across from where Martin and Mary Beersma had built their cabin. I would always check in with Mr. Green whenever I was passing his cabin to go on one of my frequent hunting or fishing trips in that area as Mr. Green was quite elderly and lived alone. Mr. Green was always delighted to see me and would always invite me into his cabin for a cup of tea or a bowl of soup. He always expressed an interest in what I was doing, where I was going, when I would return etc. He would quite often pull out from under his cot, a huge, old rifle that appeared to have a bore of about one-half inch in diameter to show me as he knew that I was quite interested in such things. As I was sitting, fondling and admiring this old rifle one fall day, Mr. Green suddenly said to me, "I don't know what size bullets it shoots but take it home with you, it's yours to keep."

I could scarcely believe my ears but away I went home with my newly acquired old rifle. Once home, I examined, cleaned and oiled up the old weapon so that everything on it was shiny, clean and appeared to work as it was intended. The rifle was about five feet long with a full-length wood stock and a tubular magazine. Barrel markings indicated that the rifle was a "Mauser" but its caliber was unclear to me.

As I felt that I just had to be able to fire this old rifle, I first had find out what its caliber was. Rationing that since it was a Mauser that its caliber was probably measured in millimeters, I found an old wooden school ruler that had markings in both inches and in millimeters. I had soon estimated, after measuring the rifle's bore about ten or more times, that it measured about eleven millimeters in diameter.

Once I had accumulated a few dollars and was in town, I went into a hardware store and asked the clerk for a box of eleven-millimeter bullets. Much to my surprise, the clerk produced a box of twenty cartridges with the words, "Eleven MM" and "43 Mauser" printed on it. Figuring that this was probably as good as it was going to get, I paid the clerk and left the store.

Once I was home I looked in detail at the box. The cartridges were about three and a half inches long with a solid lead bullet that, according to the information on the box, weighed three-hundred and eighty grains. I apprehensively inserted one of the big cartridges into the rifle chamber and found to my surprise that it fit quite nicely. I then inserted four or five more of the shells into the rifle's tubular magazine and again, found that they fit quite nicely. As the only thing left to do was to attempt to "test fire" the old rifle, I thought long and hard about just how I was going to safely perform this "test firing." It finally came to me. I went over to the woodshed, chambered a cartridge in the rifle, held it outside the shed's door that I was standing safely behind, pointed the rifle towards the old barn to the north of our house, and pulled the trigger. After the deafening roar had subsided, I checked over my hands and arms and discovering they were still attached to my body, checked over the big rifle. It was fine and I was fine. I had successfully, with a old wooden school ruler established the correct caliber of Mr. Green's old Mauser.

A Father's Son

I was to have a considerable amount of fun with that old rifle for many, many years. I eventually traded it off for a twenty-two target rifle.

Chapter 30

"Pulp Logging"

When I was about fourteen years of age, the father of a local friend of mine, Mr. Green, offered me and another of my friends, Frank Ellis, summer jobs in his remote forestry camp cutting peeled pulp. This seemed to us boys to be easy money as he was paying twenty-four dollars per cord, peeled and piled with a haul road to be also roughed in. In addition, he was providing room and board in his forest camp for three dollars each per day. According to Frank's and my calculations we could easily cut, peel and pile at least two cords of pulp per day. This amount, after room and board, would leave us a daily profit of twenty-two dollars each per day. This was pretty good money in those days when a laborer's wages were averaging about a dollar-fifty per hour.

We were soon on our way with axes, a four foot "swedesaw" each, a few spare saw blades, work gloves, fly repellant and spare work clothes. Mr. Green placed us in a long narrow bunkhouse that contained about fifteen other workers, bunk-beds and a large, centrally-placed barrel-type wood heater. We soon made ourselves at home, looking about to check out the cookhouse and the smelly fly-ridden outdoor toilets' locations, and making our hard cots as comfortable as was possible. Early the next morning following our huge camp breakfast of fried eggs, bacon, sausages, hash browned potatoes, toast and coffee, Mr. Green took us out and showed us our cutting site. We were a little, to say the least, discouraged to find ourselves in the middle of what was termed a "spruce swamp." This area consisted of densely-spaced spruce and sticky balsam trees thickly branched with a average diameter of about six or seven inches. These small diameter, thickly-branched trees meant that we would have to cut down, branch, saw up, peel and pile up a lot more logs to make up a "cord" than we would have had to if the trees had been larger with fewer branches.

Frank and I lathered ourselves with fly repellant and began to work. We soon found ourselves covered in perspiration in the damp, humid, swampy forest as we labored mightily to get together our first cord of peeled four foot logs. We also soon discovered that it matter not how much repellant we slathered on our hot sweaty skin, that our perspiration soon washed it completely away. We found ourselves covered with, and inhaling many of the millions of pesky buzzing black flies that were seeking our young tasty blood.

At the end of our second day on the job, there was no doubt whatsoever, in either Frank's or my minds that being "pulp cutters" was not to be our chosen field of employment.

On the third morning in camp we advised the understanding Mr. Green that we would, on that same day, be leaving his camp and his employment. He kindly agreed to call everything "even" so Frank and I packed up our gear and walked the approximately eight miles out to the main highway to thumb a ride home, thankful that they we had even survived.

Chapter 31

"Lumber Salesman"

During my two years of school break (so to speak) when I quit school to go to work on the Ontario Northland Railway, I also worked for a old family friend, Albert Roberts, who owned a sawmill and logging operation about fifteen miles from where we lived.

Albert was the person who, earlier in my life, had purchased me a pair of steel-cleated boys logging boots that I wore with much pride, to the chagrin of my teacher, to my fourth grade school room. Albert hired me to keep his books, make up his employees payroll, print the payroll checks, do log scaling at his logging operations and to sell sawn lumber out of his sawmill/lumber yard. He also provided me with a house trailer to reside in that was located in the lumber yard along with the sawmill.

This trailer had a bedroom, bathroom and kitchen area for me to live in. It had been modified so that the living room was now the lumber yards sales and pay office, with the remainder left as living quarters. This job was quite interesting for me as it not only entailed dealing with employees and both lumber sales to locals as well as to volume customers in Southern Ontario. It also required that I travel each week with a company pick-up truck some fifty miles out to where the logging operation was in order to deliver paychecks and scale the loggers' felled trees. I always looked forward to these scaling trips as it meant I could have lunch and sometimes supper in the cook-shack with the loggers. These meals were usually quite sumptuous with the cook always preparing more than one selection per meal and much more than enough to satisfy the hungry loggers and myself. There were also normally three or four different types of pies, cookies, cakes and many other kinds of deserts to finish off ones meal.

I really enjoyed working at this job and usually stayed in the trailer on my days off rather than return home to that not quite so enjoyable family environment.

* * *

My employer would, quite often, spend a lot of time in the trailer's office with me, just relaxing and discussing his business and his plans with me.

On one occasion, after I had been working there for about seven months, Mr. Roberts was napping on the sofa that was also in the trailer's office area and I was looking through some past payroll ledgers that I had filled out earlier in my employment. As I leafed through the ledgers, I began to spot entries that had been changed with no real attempt having been made to disguise any of the changes. As I was, at that time, just a naive sixteen or seventeen year old boy who knew next to nothing about the world of business, unemployment insurance and workers' compensation fees, I blurted out to Mr. Roberts, my boss, "Who made all these changes to our payroll ledgers? They won't add up properly with all these changes."

"Put those books away and mind your own business," Mr. Roberts replied. Flabbergasted at this response, I did as he said and said nothing more to him of that matter for the remainder of that day.

I returned home that weekend, thought long and hard about what had occurred and why my employer might have made all those changes. I did have some knowledge of a previous tax evasion offence that had been committed a few years earlier by Mr. Roberts, so the following day, a Saturday, I went to Mr. Roberts home and resigned my position, giving him no reason for my resignation. I believe that Mr. Roberts knew my reason quite well.

Chapter 32

Pressure Cooker

Mother was a excellent cook insofar as basic cooking went. I can only recall one or two occasions when she attempted to prepare any kind of meal that one might call complicated. The first was a Hasenpfeffer as described in a earlier chapter where she decided to prepare a couple of the wild snowshoe hares that I had shot or snared for the family's table. As said, her Hasenpfeffer was really enjoyed by only me and my sister Doreen. The remainder of the family, including Mother, was so put off by the smell of the marinated rabbit that they could or would not even taste it. Her normal method was to either roast them or cut them up like chicken and fry them. I believe that most of us children preferred the fried method over the oven-baked. That old wood-fired cook-stove/water heater served the family quite well for over twenty five years. Once fired up and hot, Mother could do wonders with this old relic. She made the best homemade bread I have ever tasted.

The biggest problem with using the wood-fired cook-stove was that the user had only one means of controlling the amount of heat that a pot or pan received. This method was really quite simple. You just moved the pot or pan to a cooler place on the stove. This meant that a person using the stove was required to constantly attend his or her cooking or risk burning the cooking pot and its contents on the high heat put out by the stove.

Someone, and I cannot recall who that person was, loaned Mother a big pressure cooker. This cooker operated by retaining an amount of steam under pressure within the cooker. The food was placed inside the cooker with an amount of water before the lid was placed on, tightly sealing the contents. The lid contained a pressure gauge that indicated to the user what the internal pressure of the steam was. It also contained a pressure relief plug that would blow out if the internal pressure went above the rated pressure of the pot. I cannot recall just what it was that Mother decided to cook in this cooker on what was to be her first and last attempt. What I do recall is hearing a loud explosion coming from the kitchen and Mother's screams. Rushing to the kitchen, we children found Mother yelling loudly. "What do I do now?"

As was quickly obvious, Mother had placed the pot on the hottest part of the old wood stove thereby allowing the pressure inside the pot to get so high that it blew the safety relief plug completely out of the lid. The end result was that most of the contents of the cooker were splattered all over the kitchen with the majority of it now dripping from the kitchen ceiling back onto the hot wood stove. It seems that whoever loaned Mother that pressure cooker failed to tell her that she had to keep moving the pot around on the stove to prevent excessive pressure from building up inside the pot.

For some weird and forever unexplained reason, Mother never again attempted to cook a meal by using a pressure cooker again.

Chapter 33

The Last Straw

When I returned home to the farm after my one and one-half year absence after I quit school to go working with Bill Walker on the Ontario Northland Railway, I found that Father's tormenting, abuse and put downs had increased substantially. He seemed to revel in the fact that I, now a sixteen-year-old boy, could not make a good living on my own and had to return and live "under his roof," as he put it.

As I now had some worldly experience away from Father and his influence, I refused to tolerate his slurs and putdowns as I had previously done. I now stood up to him much more than I had done previously. The culmination to Father's verbal and physical abuse came late one day when I told him that I was not going to do something that he was insisting I do. As I turned to go up the stairway to my bedroom, Father grabbed a stick of firewood from behind the kitchen stove and came up the stairs after me, intending to beat me with it.

My first warning of what was about to occur came from Mother, who yelled, "Bobby, watch out, your father is behind you". I turned at the top of the stairs, looked down at Father and said to him, "Don't come any closer or you will regret it".

Father continued up towards me with the stick raised to strike, as I stood there waiting. When he neared me, but before he could strike at me, I swung my right fist at him, striking him directly on his jaw. Father fell backwards, tumbling down the stairwell to land on his back, fortunately uninjured (other than for his pride) on the kitchen floor.

I leapt down after him and standing over him said, "I would not get up if I were you." Father wisely lay where he was until I turned and went back upstairs.

* * *

Father, after that eventful day long ago, never again touched me.

Chapter 34

"Reflections"

While it was not my intention in A Father's Son to dwell at length on the various abuses that our mother, my siblings and I suffered during the morning of our lives, I do believe that it must be mentioned, if for no other reason than to clarify just what the nature, and the end result of the abuse was.

The mental abuse for me began when Father, returning from the war, chose to ignore me, his four-year-old son, whom he had never seen. I, on that long ago day, stood proudly on the railway platform with my Mother and older sister, awaiting the arrival of my soldier father, only to be completely ignored by him. Unaware at the tender age of four years that he did not think that I was his blood son, I could not even begin to understand why he ignored me.

During my early years on the farm, I cannot recall anything really good about our life. All of my recollections surround the lack of affection, lack of care, the lack of sharing of knowledge or the showing of any sign whatsoever that our father cared at all for us. I only knew that I was there to serve him in whatever manner he desired. I can recall very few, if any, incidents or days of actual pleasure or fun during those early years where Father was directly or indirectly involved. My main memories of those early childhood farm days were days of working, physical abuse, arguing, cursing, neglect, name calling and putdowns. Nothing I ever did was done correctly or quickly enough to satisfy Father sufficiently to gain a word of praise.

It was not until I began going to a public school and performed tasks for others that I realized that at least some of the things that I did were okay, and in some cases even better than okay. I am unsure of when the actual physical abuses began but it was probably quite soon after our family's arrival on the farm. A few of my recollections of the physical and mental abuses as well as the neglect are as follows:

- Of sliding down the hill in front of our house at about five years of age on my sled, hitting and breaking my nose on a old wrecked upturned car's running board and being told "You're not hurt, so don't bother me, go tell your mother."
- Of nearly slicing my thumb off with a chisel and being told to "Go wash it off and have your mother put a bandage on it"
- Of falling through the horse-drawn hay wagon's wooden rack, knocking myself unconscious and then coming to hear Father laughing outrageously at my misfortune and telling me to, "Get up and get back to work."
- Of being unable to, at four years of age, to keep pace with Father on a long walk and then being left alone on a remote rural trail.
- Of having a pitchfork stuck in my shin at about six years of age because i was unable to work as hard or as fast as Father.
- Of being kicked in my shins at about seven or eight years of age with steel-toed boots because I was unable to work as fast as Father.
- Of being hit on the chin by Father's fist when all I wanted was for my father to show me that he cared for me.

- Of being hit on my body with sticks of firewood or kindling wood.
- Of being hit on countless occasions with Fathers leather belt.
- Of being called a "no good bastard" on more occasions than I can recall.
- Of watching Father physically and mentally abuse Mother.
- Of watching Father ignore our pleadings for help as the pet farm dog aborted her puppies and perished from Father's wolf poisoning efforts.
- Of observing Father's total, "So what" attitude upon hearing that his son Don may have ingested some of that same deadly wolf poison.
- Of seeing my father's "Let him be" attitude when a family friend, Mathew Dawson fell, unconscious and drunk, outside in the snow, in thirty degree below zero weather.
- Of having to use physical force to take a steel claw hammer from my father's hands as he was about to strike Mother with it.
- Of arriving home to find Father had taken my fishing gear and my hard-earned live bait knowing that I would wish to use them myself.
- Of even considering the shooting and killing of my father to save myself further torment at his hands.
- Of having to listen to close relatives whisper that I was my father's "bastard" son and the constant wondering of just who my father really was.
- Of having to watch Father slice the throats of farm pigs after hanging them by their severed leg tendons - while they were fully awake and conscious.

- Of having to watch Father attempt to kill the farm fowl by penetrating their brains with an "especially designed killing knife" and then having to retrieve the numerous wounded and maimed birds for the "finishing off" by twisting their bleeding heads off.
- Of having to hear, constantly, that no matter what I did, it was not done well enough or fast enough.
- Of never receiving any thanks or acknowledgement for anything that I did.
- Of never receiving any advice, instruction or assistance in things I was required to perform even though Father knew how to perform them.
- Of the fact that I had to get friends of the family to show me how to do things that my father should have shown me.
- Of having to tell Mother that her children would have been much better off in foster homes.
- Of the beatings that I received for doing something another sibling had done.
- Of the beatings that Doreen received simply because I was being beaten.
- Of the promise of being given eighty acres of land and then having Father sell it when he first could.
- Of having to strike Father with my fist to save myself from his abuse.
- Of hearing that Father has told my younger siblings that our mother is a "whore."
- Of hearing that Father had fed my newly acquired pet baby chipmunk to the family cat in order to amuse himself.

A Father's Son

Chapter 35

Remembering

The Footprint:

I remember well the time when I was guiding a excitable American bear hunter who was not having any success. Figuring to give this individual a little excitement on his hunt, Harold and I undertook to make a plaster cast of a huge bear paw. We took this cast and made impressions of a bear walking about in the sand near a bait we had set out. We then brought the American hunter to the spot and then had to listen for days about the huge bear that was consuming his bait. Unfortunately it seemed that the unseen bear only ate his bait when he, the hunter was not present. He never did catch sight of it! (We boys never, for fear of our lives, told him of our deception)

The Knife:

I recall the day when Doreen and I, alone in the house, were arguing with Doreen getting quite angry. We were in the kitchen area at the time so in her anger she picked up a table knife and hurled it at myself with all her strength. It stuck in the doorway beside my head, missing me by the narrowest of margins. Doreen was in her bare feet at the time but I still chased her down the rough gravel road for a goodly distance before giving up the chase. I never did get even with her for that incident but I am certain her bare feet must have surely suffered on that old gravel roadway.

B-52 Bomber:

I can recall the day Harold and I were flying into the lake where we were to spend a few days fishing. As the pilot was making his approach turn to land on the remote lake the small plane was buffeted by the turbulence caused by an huge low-flying American B-52 Bomber as it flew past no more than a few hundred feet below us scaring the wits out of Harold, me and the pilot. We found out later that the U. S. Air Force was permitted to practice low-level flying and navigation in that area.

Driver Training:

As my father refused to teach me to drive, I asked Sam Austen, Harold's stepdad if he would teach me. I had only driven a farm tractor but never a car prior to this time. Sam let me drive his huge Ford station wagon down the eleven or so miles to Englehart where the driver tester had me drive around the block and then parallel park. Without further ado he then issued me my driver's license.

Morel Soup:

Mother made the world's best mushroom soup with the wild morel mushrooms that grew on the farm until one day Iasked her why she had used so much pepper in it. "I did not put any pepper in it, only salt." was her reply. It was only after close scrutiny that we discovered that the "pepper" was, inn reality, tiny fleas that had came out of the mushrooms during the cooking process to "flavor" the soup during its making. Needless to say, that was the end of the morel soup making.

The Hat:

I believe it was just before Father returned from the war that Mother, Doreen and I were to visit Mom's dad and stepmother who then lived in Toronto. Mom's stepbrother, Larry took Doreen and myself to the Canadian National Exibition one day so that we could all enjoy the fair. I can quite clearly recall, as we passed near the big roller-coaster ride, seeing a man's hat floating down from the high ride as it passed far overhead. What I did not see, and did not realize, was that the male owner of the hat had also fallen from the ride, dying from the impact. I was told this by Uncle Larry many years later.

"The Nickel":

I shall always remember the time before our Dad came home from the war when we still living in New Liskeard. It was a hot humid summers day when Doreen and I attempted to convince Mother to give us a nickel so that we could go down to the corner store and buy ourselves an ice-cream cone. Mother would not relent so we checked out her dresser and discovered a solitary nickel lying in plain sight. We were soon back home, sharing the ice cream cone that we had purchased after "liberating" that nickel. Our enjoyment, however, soon came to an end when Mother spotted us licking away on that shared delicious ice cream cone. She sat us both down, and as our punishment for stealing that nickel, made us watch her as she finished eating the cone herself. A lesson well taught and forever remembered!

Pet Mink:

When I was living and working for Harold's stepdad Sam at the Northern Ontario Wildlife park, I purchased, for five dollars, a tiny baby mink that someone had picked up from the roadside. This little fellow was only about five or six inches long, (tail included) and was the cutest thing you ever saw. He was as tame as could be and I used to carry him around in my shirt pocket where he would curl up and occasionally stick his head out to check on his surroundings. As he grew I would place him on the ground where he would follow me around like a pet puppy. He was, as I soon found out, afraid of water and just hated to get wet. Wildlife officials told me that what I had done was impossible. They said that no-one could 'tame' a wild mink. Unfortunately, I found the little creature dead in his pen one day when he was about three months old.

"Lassie":

I remembers how our beautiful Lassie would, with a simple "Lassie, go get the cows," range as far out as was necessary from our home to fetch the cows home for the evening milking. She never failed to bring them home no matter how far they had roamed during the day.

"Blueberry Bear":

I vividly remember picking blueberries with Mother one summer day on the rocks behind the farm when I was about eight years old. As I was crouched down picking away, I could hear Mother rustling about nearby as she picked. After a few minutes of talking to her with no response, I stood-up to get a look at just where she was. At about the same time I stood up, the large black bear (that I had thought was Mother) that had been feeding voraciously on the blueberries a few feet from me also stood up on his hind feet to see what all the ruckus was about. Needless to say it did not take me very long to find Mother.

Chapter 36

Regrets

Frank's Partridge:

I do still remember and regret that I did not give Frank the first shot at the partridge that was sitting in the tree above his head. I have never forgotten he look that Frank gave me when I shot the bird as Frank was aiming at it with his little four-ten shotgun and about to fire."Sorry, I owe you one, Frank."

Richard Dumas:

I regret not having the courage to let Richard Dumas know how I felt about him the last time I saw him alive. Richard was, at the time, in an advanced stage of Parkinson's and had very little control of himself. His fly was open, his boots were not laced, his shirt was undone, he was unshaven and I just said hello, how are you, etc. etc. Richard was more of a father to me than my real father. I truly regret not telling him that. I miss you, Richard.

Darren:

I regret telling my brother Darren that he had to leave our home and that we could no longer afford to keep and feed him when he came to us on the Queen Charlotte Islands in obvious pain. I had no excuse for that, Darren, please forgive me.

Father:

I regret that I have been unable to forgive you for what you did and did not do for me, for my brothers and sisters and to our mother. Even though I realize that my inability to forgive you only harms myself, it matters not. I have tried but I cannot forgive you.

Harold

Although you may not remember the incident, I regret what I said when I saw you for the first time in many years. I was in a very depressed state at the time and do not know why, but when I saw you walking across the field with Sam, I recall shouting at you from a distance something like, "Sam, who is that fat person walking with you?". I sincerely apologize to you, Harold, you were and are still, a true and loyal friend.

"Blame":

I sincerely regret having said to Mother one day while she was in the presence of Barb Lott, that we children would have been better off during our childhood if she had left Dad and placed us in foster homes. While this may very well have been true, it hurt her very much. I now realize that those early years probably hurt her as much or more than they hurt me.

Forgiving:

Last, but not least, and perhaps the most important of all, is that I truly regret that I have been unable to, even after all these years, to forgive our father, who instead of providing a healthy family environment that would enhance the growth and positive development of all of his children, created a home full of hate, mistrust, pain and despair. Unfortunately, my inability to forgive Father has probably done me more harm than it could possibly do to him. "A wonderful legacy, Father!"

Chapter 37

Finally

Looking back at my years on that Mindoka homestead and my subsequent life, there are a few things that I can say with some certainty really affected my life greatly after Mindoka. These same things, in all probability, also affected my siblings to a lesser or to possibly a greater degree. The worst thing that happened, (that I can now see quite clearly) is the fact that none of the children were shown or taught how to love themselves or anyone else. Being devoid of this ability, or unable to even feel or show any emotion other than anger or disappointment can and does create an incurable, life-long cancer within oneself. The physical abuses, while they may be painful to the body at the time they occur, are soon long forgotten, whereas the internal scars, the mental abuses and traumas remain with us forever.

I believe that most, if not all of the children of our family are very much like our deceased brother Don, who, in my perspective, spent his entire short life searching -- searching for what we children all lacked during our childhood: love. Most of all, we were left without the ability to truly care and to love others. The most terrible of all, we were left without the ability to teach our own children how to love. Unfortunately for our children, this heavy cross is one that their own children may now be forced to bear.

***

My final comments to myself concerning Father's treatment of me are:

"Sorry, Dad, I can think of nothing good to say of you. Your attempts in the latter years of your life to obtain my forgiveness only served to confirm to me that you were always quite well aware of what you were doing to me at the time. Even now, after all these years, your abuses are still having their effect."

I still, at times, wonder if I should have, on that sunny fall day long ago, squeezed that trigger on my rifle just a little more. I am, however, for the most part, glad that I did stay my shot.

~ * ~

When I was in the mid-years of my life, my wife—the mother of my two children, Jon and Dianne—left and took from me my children. I then entered a stage of depression that nearly caused me to take my own life. Instead of taking this action, I chose to seek mental counseling for the grief of losing my children and to, hopefully permit me to continue my life in a more rational and "normal" manner. This counseling required me, as part of my therapy, to forgive in writing both Mother and Father for what they did or did not do to me.

I was, as a result, able to finally understand and forgive anything that I might have blamed Mother for.

Unfortunately, I was not, and could not do the same with regards to Father. I twice went to visit Father's gravesite in an effort to forgive. On both of these occasions I left after considerable meditation but no forgiveness was forthcoming.

I do realize that it is only me that I am hurting by not forgiving Father but I cannot do so even though I realize it might help him in the healing process. The writing of this book will hopefully assist in my healing.

A Father's Son

"THE END"(Or possibly just the beginning ?)

www.ingramcontent.com/pod-product-compliance
Lightning Source LLC
Chambersburg PA
CBHW060133100426
42744CB00007B/773